TABLE OF INDEX

TABLE OF INDEX

INSTRUCTIONS

The answers to each problem is in the back of this book, section 100.0.   I think it is best for the parents to remove this part of the book.

Calculators Are allowed only on question starting with the number four, or the Geometry section

The problems might not be in sequential order.   Don't worry its correct.

\# If you don't get the correct answer, and want an explanation on how to work the problem, go to youtube and type in "MMT" then the problem number. An example would be "MMT 3.9.w12" The video will show you how to work problem 3.9.w12.

\# For one on one tutoring via skype at $35.00/Hr.; contact me at marksmathtutoring@yahoo.com

REFERENCES

LENGTH

ENGLISH

1 mile (mi) = 1,760 yards (yds)
1 yard (yd) = 3 feet (ft)
1 foot (ft) = 12 inches (in)

METRIC

1 kilometer (km) = 1,000 meters (m)
1 meter (m) = 100 centimeters (cm)
1 centimeters (cm) = 10 millimeters (mm)

VOLUME AND CAPACITY

ENGLISH

1 gallon (gal) = 4 quarts (gt)
1 quart (qt) = 2 pints (pt)
1 pint (pt) = 2 cups (c)
1 cup © = 8 fluid ounces (fl oz)

METRIC

1 liter = 1,000 millimeters (ml)

WEIGHT AND MASS

ENGLISH

1 ton (T) = 2,000 pounds (lb)
1 pound (lb) = 16 ounces (oz)

METRIC

1 kilogram (kg) = 1,000 grams (g)
1 gram (g) = 1,000 milligrams (mg)

TIME

1 year = 12 months
1 year = 52 weeks
1 week = 7 days
1 day = 24 hours
1 hour = 60 minutes
1 minute = 60 seconds

REFERENCES

PERIMETER

Square   4 X SIDE = PERIMETER

Rectangle   LENGTH + LENGTH + SIDE + SIDE = PERIMETER

AREA

Square   SIDE X SIDE = AREA

Rectangle   LENGTH X SIDE = AREA

Croquis of a Deliberate Crime

YouTube

If you don't get the correct answer, and want an explanation on how to work the problem, go to YouTube and type in "MMT" then the problem number. An example would be, MMT 3.9.w12,. The video will show you how to work problem 3.9.w12.

For one on one tutoring via skype at $35.00/Hr.; contact me at marksmathtutoring@yahoo.com

DEFINITIONS

Sum is the answer after adding the numbers

Product is the answer after dividing the numbers

Difference is the answer after subtracting the numbers

Congruent means if two shapes have the same shape and size of each other. They don't need two have the same orientation. In other words one can be up side down from the other.

Lines of symmetry is a line that divides a shape into two equal size and shape. Two examples are shown below

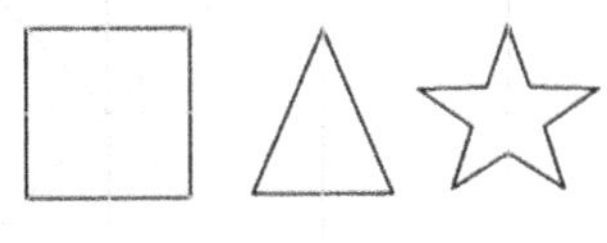

Serza is a 7 sided figure. It is also called a heptagone. Example is below.

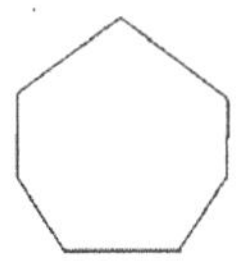

Rhombus is a figure with four side all of equal length. All Rhombuses are parallelograms and kites. A square is a Rhombus with all 90 degree angle. A diamond, or kite shape is also a Rhombus. Two example are below.

Square is a parallelogram with 4 right angle (90 degrees), or a Quadrilaterals with 4 right angles with four sides of equal length

Kite: Is a Rhombus with angles that are not right angles (90 degrees)

Parallelogram has two sets of parallel lines. The opposite sides are of equal length.

Trapezoid four sided figure with one set of parallel sides.

Rectangle is a parallelogram with 4 right angle (90 degrees), or said another way a Quadrilaterals with 4 right angles

Polygons is a figure that would lie flat on a table. It is made up of straight lines and is closed, or could be used to contain your dog like a fence. Any shape will do as long as it is flat and closed, or no open gates in the fence.

Quadrilaterals Is a polygon with four side and four edges. The following are some examples

Pentagons is a five sided polygon

Hexagons is a six sided polygon. Example is below

Vertices means corner.

Edge is a line where two planes or sheet meet. Where the wall joins to the flour is a edge.

Even is a whole number that is divisible by two. The best way at your age to determine this is start with 2 and count up by 2s. Ex 2, 4, 6, 8, 10, etc. If you say the number it is even.

Odd whole number that is not even. The last digit of the number is a 1,3,5,7,or a 9. Examples of add number would ne 221, 683, 66889, or 7.

ONES PLACE: is the place holding the smallest value. The underlined bold number is in the ones place in these examples: 2**4**, 34**6**, 48**6**, 126**7**, 32**5**, 67**9**,1125**8**

TENS PLACE: IS the smallest value that can divided by 10 evenly. The underlined bold number is in the tens place in these examples: 2**3**6, **4**5, 57**7**8, 825**7**8, **5**4, 1**2**8, 7**7**8

HUNDREDS PLACE: TENS PLACE: IS the smallest value that can divided by 100 evenly. The underlined bold number is in the hundreds place in these examples: **1**27, 3**4**67, 5**7**88, 3**2**75, **3**46

THOUSANDS PLACE: IS the smallest value that can divided by 1000 evenly. The underlined bold number is in the THOUSANDS place in these examples: **3**276, 4**5**887, **2**457, 11**1**278, 12**2**895

Interest Is the extra money you pay back. If you borrow $200 and pay back $210, the interest is $10.

Units of weight: pounds, grams, ounces, tones

Units of volume: Gallons, quarts, pints

Units of Length: Centimeter (cm), Millimeter (mm), Meter (m), Kilometer, Inch (in), Foot (ft), Mile

GREATER THAN: Uses the symbol **>** It mean the item on the left is greater than the item on the right. An example would be 8>3. In words this is eight is greater than 3. Remember the bird always eats the bigger worm.

LESS THAN: Uses the symbol **<** It mean the item on the left is less than the item on the right. An example would be 8<3. In words this is eight is greater than 3. Remember the bird always eats the bigger worm.

GREATER THAN OR EQUAL TO: Uses the symbol **≥** It mean the item on the left is greater than or equal to the item on the right. An example would be 8≥8. In words this is eight is greater than or equal to 8. Remember the bird always eats the bigger worm.

LESS THAN OR EQUAL TO: Uses the symbol **≤** It mean the item on the left is less than or equal to the item on the right. An example would be 8≤8. In words this is eight is greater than or equal to 8. Remember the bird always eats the bigger worm.

Croquis of a
Deliberate
Crime

YouTube

If you don't get the correct answer, and want an explanation on how to work the problem, go to YouTube and type in "MMT" then the problem number. An example would be, MMT 3.9.w12,. The video will show you how to work problem 3.9.w12.

For one on one tutoring via skype at $35.00/Hr.; contact me at marksmathtutoring@yahoo.com

2.0 LOGIC

2.1) What would be the best unit of measurement for the size of your dog?
a) Gallons, b) pounds, c) pints, d) Quart

2.2) You parents borrowed $5,000.00 from the bank to buy a car. They repaid $6,500.00. Which statement best explains why they paid the extra $1,500.00
a) They wanted to donate $1,500.00 to the bank to be nice
b) They repaid the loan on a week day and the bank charges money for these days
c) They had extra money and nothing to do with it.
d) The bank charged $1,500.00 in interest for a $6,000.00 loan

2.3) I'm thinking of a number. It has a 3 in the thousands place and a 4 in the hundreds place Which of the following could be the number I am think about?
a) 1,356
b) 3,247
c) 3,456
d) 4,389

2.4) I'm thinking of a number. It has a 4 in the thousands place and a 5 in the tens place. Which of the following could be the number I am think about?
a) 2,557
b) 1376
c) 4,157
d) 6578

2.5) I'm thinking of a number. It has a 2 in the tens place and a 7 in the ones place. Which of the following could be the number I am thinking about?
a) 137
b) 27
c) 331
d) 72

2.6) I'm thinking of a number. It has a 6 in the thousands place and a 8 in the ones place. Which of the following could be the number I am thinking about?
a) 8,236
b) 5,468
c) 4,648
d) 6,458

2.7) What number is in the hundreds palace of 137

2.8) What number is in the thousands place of 7,689

2.29) Which of the following has the same value of 6,315,256
a)6,000,000+300,000+5,000,+200+50+6
b)6,000,000+300,000+10,000+200+50+6
c)6,000,000+300,000+10,000+5,000,+200
d)6,000,000+300,000+10,000+5,000,+200+50+6

2.30) Which of the following has the same value of 140,312
a)100,000+140,000+3000+10+2
b) 1,400,000+40,000+300+10+2
c) 100,000+40,000+10+2
d) 100,000+40,000+300+10+2

2.9) What is the relationship between the hundreds place and the tens place in the number 4,221
a) The hundreds place is 2 times larger than the tens place
b) The hundreds place is 1 more than the tens place
c) The hundreds place is 10 times the tens place
d) There is no relationship between them.

2.10) What is the relationship between the thousands place and the hundreds place in the number 4,411
a) The hundreds place is 2 times larger than the tens place
b) The hundreds place is 1 more than the tens place
c) The hundreds place is 10 times the tens place
d) There is no relationship between them.

2.11) Which statement about the number 48 is true
a) It is odd, because it can be divided by 3
b) It is even, because it can be divided by 2
c) It is even because 8+4=12 is even
d) It is even because 4 and 8 are both even

2.12) Which of the following numbers is even
a) 27, b) 32, c) 81, d) 127

2.13) Which of the following numbers is even
a) 236, b) 137, c) 5179, d) 331

2.14) Which of the following numbers is odd
a) 24, b) 377, c) 6428, d) 46

2.15) Which of the following numbers is odd
a) 45, b) 224, c) 56, d) 2246

2.16) Which of the following numbers is even
a) 2278, b) 321, c) 56797, d) 33

2.17) Which of the following numbers is odd
a) 3357, b) 324, a) 32, d) 124

2.18) Loren has six football jerseys hanging on the wall. Which ones are even numbered?

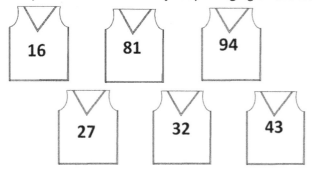

2.19) I am thinking of a number. There are three clues below.

    # The value of the digit 7 is (7X100)

    # The value of the digit 6 is (6X10)

    # The value of the digit 3 is (3X1)

Which of the following number could be the number I am thinking about

a) 367

b) 673

c) 763

d) 736

2.20) I am thinking of a number. There are three clues below.

    # The value of the digit 5 is (5X1000)

    # The value of the digit 5 is (5X10)

    # The value of the digit 4 is (4X1)

Which of the following number could be the number I am thinking about

a) 5054

b) 5145

c) 4154

d) 5545

2.21) A book has the weight of 3 kilograms. Which of the following could have the same mass.
a) a car, b) airplane, c) peanut, d) small cat

2.35) What would be the best unit of measurement for the distance between you and your school?
a) Gallons, b) miles, c) pints, d) feet

2.36) What would be the best unit of measurement for the amount of milk in your refrigerator?
a) Gallons, b) pounds, c) miles, d) feet

2.37) What would be the best unit of measurement for the distance between you and your TV?
a) Gallons, b) pounds, c) pints, d) feet

3.0 ARITHMETIC

3.1 Addition-Single Digits

3.1.1) 1+3=	3.1.2) 2+0=	3.1.3) 4+6=	3.1.4) 5+8=	3.1.5) 3+2=	3.1.6) 7+3=
3.1.7) 3+0=	3.1.8) 7+9=	3.1.9) 1+8=	3.1.10) 5+5=	3.1.11) 7+4=	3.1.12) 2+6=
3.1.13) 4+5=	3.1.14) 5+9=	3.1.15) 2+5=	3.1.16) 6+9=	3.1.17) 4+2=	3.1.18) 3+8=
3.1.19) 2+2=	3.1.20) 4+8=	3.1.21) 8+2=	3.1.22) 9+5=	3.1.23) 6+4=	3.1.24) 8+5=
3.1.25) 4+7=	3.1.26) 8+7=	3.1.27) 9+9=	3.1.28) 9+0=	3.1.29) 6+6=	3.1.30) 2+7=
3.1.31) 1+2=	3.1.32) 7+8=	3.1.33) 6+2=	3.1.34) 3+4=	3.1.35) 9+4=	3.1.36) 1+5=
3.1.37) 7+6=	3.1.38) 8+8=	3.1.39) 9+6=	3.1.40) 1+6=	3.1.41) 6+5=	3.1.42) 9+2=

3.1.43) 7 +3	3.1.44) 9 +4	3.1.45) 3 +6	3.1.46) 5 +9	3.1.47) 8 +5	3.1.48) 5 +7
3.1.49) 8 +8	3.1.50) 7 +2	3.1.51) 6 +4	3.1.52) 7 +7	3.1.53) 3 +2	3.1.54) 2 +9

3.2 Addition-Two Digits

3.2.1)11+23=	3.2.2)22+20=	3.2.3)34+16=	3.2.4)65+68=	3.2.5)83+22=	3.2.6)33+60=
3.2.7)17+39=	3.2.8)81+48=	3.2.9)65+05=	3.2.10)37+74=	3.2.11)34+25=	3.2.12)85+39=
3.2.13)72+35=	3.2.14)16+49=	3.2.15)44+92=	3.2.16)92+12=	3.2.17)44+28=	3.2.18)28+32=
3.2.19)19+55=	3.2.20)36+54=	3.2.21)84+67=	3.2.22)98+27=	3.2.23)29+59=	3.2.24)19+40=
3.2.25)36+66=	3.2.26)11+62=	3.2.27)47+38=	3.2.28)76+12=	3.2.29)23+64=	3.2.30)79+54=
3.2.31)37+46=	3.2.32)18+88=	3.2.33)79+26=	3.2.34)31+56=	3.2.35)26+85=	3.2.36) 40+31=

3.2.37) 21 +34	3.2.38) 57 +56	3.2.39) 89 +32	3.2.40) 65 +67	3.2.41) 81 +83	3.2.42) 51 +17
3.2.43) 75 +46	3.2.44) 67 +76	3.2.45) 32 +88	3.2.46) 99 +37	3.2.47) 27 +28	3.2.48) 31 +98

3.3 Sub Section Multiple Digit Addition

3.3.1)111+2365=	3.3.2)2227+201=	3.3.3)343+160	3.3.4)165+6825=
3.3.5)8301+22=	3.3.6)331+602=	3.3.7)1775+39=	3.3.8)811+483=
3.3.9)6523+105=	3.3.10)376+742=	3.3.11)345+255=	3.3.12)854+399=
3.3.13)726+355=	3.3.14)116+949=	3.3.15)44+192=	3.3.16)920+128=
3.3.17)445+287=	3.3.18)284+132=	3.3.19)119+855=	3.3.20)336+254=
3.3.21)284+367=	3.3.22)298+727=	3.3.23)29+2259=	3.3.24)119+409=
3.3.25)365+166=	3.3.26)110+627=	3.3.27)475+386=	3.3.28)768+129=
3.3.29)236+642=	3.3.30)790+543=	3.3.31)375+461=	3.3.32)182+888=
3.3.33)793+265=	3.3.34)314+5611=	3.3.35)2664+8551=	3.3.36)21+568=

3.3.37) 571 +343	3.3.38) 2889 +566	3.3.39) 1653 +327	3.3.40) 781 +679	3.3.41) 3256 +124

3.3.42) 245 +31	3.3.43) 175 +46	3.3.44) 267 +376	3.3.45) 132 +988	3.3.46) 199 +337

The table below shows the number of dogs with each color in a small town.

Color of dogs	Number of dogs
Black	215
white	167
yellow	132
brown	367
spotted	197

3.3.w1) How many dogs live in this small town?

3.3.w2) What is the total number of black, white and brown dogs living in this small town?

3.3.w3) How many spotted dogs live in this small town?

3.3.w4) What is the total number of brown and yellow dogs living in this small town?

The following table lists the number of lakes in each state

State	Number of Lakes
Illinois	23
Washington	71
California	82
Arizona	17
Kentucky	45
New York	67

3.3.w5) How many lakes are there in California?

3.3.w6) How many lakes are there in Arizona?

3.3.w7) What is the total number of lakes in Arizona, Kentucky and New York?

3.3.w8) What is the total number of lakes listed in this table?

The following lists the number of vegetables Mary grew in her garden this year
    # onions 346
    #carrots 157
    #tomatoes 281

3.3.w9) How many carrots did Mary grow?

3.3.w10) What is the total number of vegetables Mary grew?

3.3.w11)What is the total number of onions and tomatoes that Mary grew?

The following is a series of numbers
    6, 10, 14, 18

3.3.w12) What would be the next two numbers in this series

3.3.w13) What number would not be in this series?
    a) 30, b) 38, c) 44, d) 50

3.3.w14) Which number represents the number 674
    a) 200+400+65+9
    b) 60+7+4
    c) 342+472
    d) 60+70+40

3.3.w15) You open a bank account with $127. The next week you deposit $312, followed by another $251 the next week. What is the amount in your bank account?

3.3.w16) I bought 1 cake for $12.83 and two pies for $15.61 each. What was the total cost of this purchase?

3.3.w17) The following table details the number of apples the school sold last week. What is the best estimate of the total number of apples sold last week?

DAY	NUMBER
Monday	132
Tuesday	247
Wednesday	331
Thursday	287
Friday	198

3.3.w22) If the rule is add 48 to a number to get the answer which table below shows this relationship?

A)

NUMBER	EXPRESSION	ANSWER
48	48+1	49
48	48+2	50
48	48+3	51
48	48-4	52

B)

NUMBER	EXPRESSION	ANSWER
48	48x1	48
48	48-1	48
48	48+0	48
48	48-0	48

C)

NUMBER	EXPRESSION	ANSWER
1	1+48	49
2	2+48	50
3	3+48	51
4	4+48	52

d)

NUMBER	EXPRESSION	ANSWER
1	35+1	36
2	36+2	38
3	37+3	40
4	38+4	42

3.3.w23) A bakery makes 500 chocolate cupcakes per day . They make 135 more vanilla cupcakes per day than chocolate. Which equation below could be used to find X the total number of vanilla cupcakes per day.
a) x=500-135
b)x= 500+135
c) x= 500X135
d) x=500÷135

3.3.w24) The table below shows the number of apples compared with the number of oranges

APPLES	ORANGES
82	114
95	127
64	96
47	79
78	110

Which statement below best described the relationship between apples and oranges
a) apples + 32 = oranges
b) apples – 32 = oranges
c) oranges +32 = apples
d) oranges + apples = 32

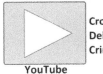

Croquis of a
Deliberate
Crime

YouTube

3.4 Subtraction-Single Digits

3.4.1) 5-3=   3.4.2) 2-0=   3.4.3) 8-6=   3.4.4) 9-8=   3.4.5) 3-2=   3.4.6) 7-3=
3.4.7) 3-0=   3.4.8) 7-4=   3.4.9) 1-1=   3.4.10) 5-4=   3.4.11) 7-4=   3.4.12) 2-1=
3.4.13) 4-3=   3.4.14) 5-4=   3.4.15) 2-1=   3.4.16) 6-3=   3.4.17) 4-3=   3.4.18) 9-8=
3.4.19) 2-2=   3.4.20) 4-1=   3.4.21) 8-2=   3.4.22) 9-5=   3.4.23) 6-4=   3.4.24) 8-5=
3.4.25) 4-3=   3.4.26) 8-7=   3.4.27) 9-9=   3.4.28) 9-0=   3.4.29) 6-6=   3.4.30) 9-7=
3.4.31) 9-2=   3.4.32) 9-8=   3.4.33) 6-2=   3.4.34) 8-4=   3.4.35) 9-4=   3.4.36) 8-5=
3.4.37) 7-6=   3.4.38) 8-8=   3.4.39) 9-6=   3.4.40) 9-6=   3.4.41) 6-5=   3.4.42) 9-2=

3.4.43) 7	3.4.44) 9	3.4.45) 8	3.4.46) 9	3.4.47) 8	3.4.48) 9
-3	-4	-6	-9	-5	-7

3.4.49) 8	3.4.50) 7	3.4.51) 6	3.4.52) 7	3.4.53) 3	3.4.54) 8
-8	-2	-4	-7	-2	-6

3.5 Subtraction-Two Digits

3.5.1)81-23=   3.5.2)22-20=   3.5.3)34-16=   3.5.4)65-28=   3.5.5)83-22=   3.5.6)33-20=
3.5.7)97-39=   3.5.8)81-48=   3.5.9)65-05=   3.5.10)87-74=   3.5.11)34-25=   3.5.12)85-39=
3.5.13)72-5=   3.5.14)56-49=   3.5.15)44-12=   3.5.16)92-2=   3.5.17)44-28=   3.5.18)88-32=
3.5.19)19-15=   3.5.20)86-54=   3.5.21)84-67=   3.5.22)98-27=   3.5.23)59-29=   3.5.24)79-40=
3.5.25)36-6=   3.5.26)61-10=   3.5.27)47-38=   3.5.28)76-2=   3.5.29)23-4=   3.5.30)79-54=
3.5.31)37-16=   3.5.32)18-9=   3.5.33)79-26=   3.5.34)31-6=   3.5.35)86-85=   3.5.36) 17-8

3.5.37) 81	3.5.38) 57	3.5.39) 89	3.5.40) 65	3.5.41) 81	3.5.42) 45
-34	- 6	-32	-47	-73	-1

3.5.43) 75	3.5.44) 67	3.5.45) 32	3.5.46) 99	3.5.47) 27	3.5.48) 67
-46	- 6	-18	-37	-18	-38

3.6 Subtraction-Multiple digit addition

3.6.1)1111-365=   3.6.2)2227-201=   3.6.3)343-160   3.6.4)165-25=   3.6.5)8301-22=
3.6.6)1331-302=   3.6.7)1775-39=   3.6.8)811-483=   3.6.9)6523-105=   3.6.10)976-742=
3.6.11)345-255=   3.6.12)854-99=   3.6.13)726-355=   3.6.14)116-49=   3.6.15)244-192=
3.6.16)920-128=   3.6.17)445-287=   3.6.18)284-12=   3.6.19)1119-855=   3.6.20)336-254=
3.6.21)284-167=   3.6.22)798-727=   3.6.23)1129-159=   3.6.24)119-9=   3.6.25)365-166=
3.6.26)1110-627=   3.6.27)475-386=   3.6.28)768-129=   3.6.29)236-42=   3.6.30)790-543=
3.6.31)875-461=   3.6.32)882-288=   3.6.33)793-265=   3.6.34)5314-611=   3.6.35)9664-8551=
3.6.36)621-568=   3.6.37)1127-89=   3.6.38)187-129=   3.6.39)327-189=   3.6.40)1321-287=

3.6.41) 571	3.6.42) 2889	3.6.43) 1653	3.6.44) 781	3.6.45) 3256	3.6.46) 321
-343	- 66	-327	-679	-124	-264

3.6.47) 245	3.6.48) 175	3.6.49) 267	3.2.50) 1132	3.2.51) 3199	3.2.52) 127
- 31	-46	- 76	-988	-337	-89

3.6.w1) Sue back 827 cookies

        #She sold 127 of the cookies

        #Her brother Mike sold 81 of the cookies

What is the best way to figure out how many cookies she has left over

      a)   827-127-81=, b) 127-827-81=, c) 827+127+81=, d) 127+81-827=

      b)   How many cookies are left over

3.6.w2) Mark picked 427 apples on Monday, the 328 pears on Tues. What is the difference between the number of apples and pears he picked?

3.6.w3)Mike goal is to mow 125 lawns this summer

        # In June he mows 35

        # In July he mows 61

How many lawns must he mow in August to make his goal?

3.6.w24) The table below shows the number of cats and dogs for three different public school

School	Cats	dogs
Harrison	126	217
Casis	118	187
Baker	153	254

What is the total difference between the number of cats and dogs?

3.6.w4)Gilbert bought 87 flowers for his moms garden. He put 31 in the front yard and 27 in the back. How many flowers did he have left?

3.6.w5)Wanda saved the following amount of money in three months

        #March she saved $827

        #April she saved $294

        # May she saved $447

How much more money did she save in March than April and May combined?

3.6.w6)Rita had two boxes of cupcakes

        #She made 85 chocolate

        #She made 76 vanilla

        #Her brother ate 28 of them

Which equation would be useful in finding the number of cupcakes she had left after her brother ate them.

a) 85+76-28=

b) 85+76+28=

c) 85-76+28=

d) 85-76-28=

How many cupcakes did she have left after her brother ate some?

3.6.w7) Sarah grew three vegetables in her garden last year. The list below shows the number of each she grew.

        # 127 tomatoes

        # 312 cucumbers

        # 187 carrots

Which expression below is the best way to determine the difference between the number of carrots and tomatoes she grew?

a) 127-187, b) 187-127, c) 187+127, d) 127+187

3.6.w8) Mike rode his bike 431 miles in June and 277 mile in July. What is the difference in miles between these two months?

3.6.w9)Larimer save $841 in April, he spent $128 in May then saved another $56 in June. Which expression is best for determining the amount of money he has saved?
a)841-128+56=
b) 841-128-56=
c)841+128+56=
d)841+56-128=

3.6.w10) Brad has 841 apples in two boxes. He has 367 in one box. How many apples are in the other box?

3.6.w11) I ate 7 more oranges than apples. Which tables below shows this relationship.

A)

APPLES	ORANGES
4	11
6	13
8	15
10	17
15	24

C)

APPLES	ORANGES
4	11
6	13
8	15
10	17
15	22

B)

APPLES	ORANGES
4	11
6	12
8	15
10	17
15	22

D)

APPLES	ORANGES
4	12
6	14
8	16
10	17
15	22

3.6.W12) If you bake 4 cupcakes on Mon, 6 on Tuesday, then 5 on Wednesday, how many cupcakes would you have?

3.6.w13) It took me three years to save $25,357. If the first year I saved $8,113, and $7,891, how much did I save in the third year?

3.6.w14) The table below shows the relationship between the miles I hiking and biking.

MONTH	BIKING	HIKING
June	28	15
July	32	19
August	35	22
September	41	28

Which equation below shows this relationship?
a) Miles biked – 13 = miles hiked
b) Miles biked - 11 = miles hiked
c) Miles biked - 12 = miles hiked
d) Miles biked - 15 = miles hiked

3.6.w15) I have two jars with penny's
Jar A has 27,315 pennies
Jar B has 8,465 pennies
What is the best estimate for the difference in the number of pennies in these two jars?

3.6.w16) I bought a bike to repair then sale. The following is the amount I spent and sold it for
Bought bike for $12.00
Repaired bike for $8.00
#Painted bike for $5.50
#sold bike for $30.00
What is the best estimate for the amount of profit I made?

3.6.w17) You sold pizza at a bake sale. The cost of making all the pizza was $10.35. They sold for a total of $21.11. What was your profit?

3.6.w18) My dog has $14.00 to spend on treats and toys. He buys on ball for $2.85, two cookies for $0.65 each, and a chew toy for $1.97. What is the amount of money he has left over?

3.6.w19) The following is a list of the number of miles I walk each month.
#June 327
#July 451
#Aug 634
If my goal was 1500, how many more do I need to walk?

3.7 Multiplication-Single Digits

3.7.1) 1x3=	3.7.2) 2x0=	3.7.3) 4x6=	3.7.4) 5x8=	3.7.5) 3x2=	3.7.6) 7x3=
3.7.7) 3x0=	3.7.8) 7x9=	3.7.9) 1x8=	3.7.10) 5x5=	3.7.11) 7x4=	3.7.12) 2x6=
3.7.13) 4x5=	3.7.14) 5x9=	3.7.15) 2x5=	3.7.16) 6x9=	3.7.17) 4x2=	3.7.18) 3x8=
3.7.19) 2x2=	3.7.20) 4x8=	3.7.21) 8x2=	3.7.22) 9x5=	3.7.23) 6x4=	3.7.24) 8x5=
3.7.25) 4x7=	3.7.26) 8x7=	3.7.27) 9x9=	3.7.28) 9x0=	3.7.29) 6x6=	3.7.30) 2x7=
3.7.31) 1x2=	3.7.32) 7x8=	3.7.33) 6x2=	3.7.34) 3x4=	3.7.35) 9x4=	3.7.36) 1x5=
3.7.37) 7x6=	3.7.38) 8x8=	3.7.39) 9x6=	3.7.40) 1x6=	3.7.41) 6x5=	3.7.42) 9x2=

3.7.43) 7 x3	3.7.44) 9 x4	3.7.45) 3 x6	3.7.46) 5 x9	3.7.47) 8 x5	3.7.48) 5 x7
3.7.49) 8 x8	3.7.50) 7 x2	3.7.51) 6 x4	3.7.52) 7 x7	3.7.53) 3 x2	3.7.54) 2 x9

Croquis of a Deliberate Crime
YouTube

If you don't get the correct answer, and want an explanation on how to work the problem, go to YouTube and type in "MMT" then the problem number. An example would be, MMT 3.9.w12,. The video will show you how to work problem 3.9.w12.

For one on one tutoring via skype at $35.00/Hr.; contact me at marksmathtutoring@yahoo.com

3.8 Multiplication-Two Digits

3.8.1)11x23=   3.8.2)22x20=   3.8.3)34x16=   3.8.4)65x68=   3.8.5)83x22=   3.8.6)33x60=

3.8.7)17x39=   3.8.8)81x48=   3.8.9)65x05=   3.8.10)37x74=   3.8.11)34x25=   3.8.12)85x39=

3.8.13)72x35=   3.8.14)16x49=   3.8.15)44x92=   3.8.16)92x12=   3.8.17)44x28=   3.8.18)28x32=

3.8.19)19x55=   3.8.20)36x54=   3.8.21)84x67=   3.8.22)98x27=   3.8.23)29x59=   3.8.24)19x40=

3.8.25)36x66=   3.8.26)11x62=   3.8.27)47x38=   3.8.28)76x12=   3.8.29)23x64=   3.8.30)79x54=

3.8.31)37x46=   3.8.32)18x88=   3.8.33)79x26=   3.8.34)31x56=   3.8.35)26x85=   3.8.36)84x16=

3.8.37) 21	3.8.38) 57	3.8.39) 89	3.8.40) 65	3.8.41) 81	3.8.42) 27
x34	x56	x32	x67	x83	x53

3.8.43) 45	3.8.44) 75	3.8.45) 67	3.8.46) 32	3.8.47) 99	3.8.48) 56
x31	x46	x76	x88	x37	x78

3.9 Sub Section Multiple digit Multiplication

3.9.1)111x2365=   3.9.2)2227x201=   3.9.3)343x160=   3.9.4)165x6825=

3.9.5)8301x22=   3.9.6)331x602=   3.9.7)1775x39=   3.9.8)811x483=

3.9.9)6523x105=   3.9.10)376x742=   3.9.11)345x255=   3.9.12)854x399=

3.9.13)726x355=   3.9.14)116x949=   3.9.15)44x192=   3.9.16)920x128=

3.9.17)445x287=   3.9.18)284x132=   3.9.19)119x855=   3.9.20)336x254=

3.9.21)284x367=   3.9.22)298x727=   3.9.23)29x2259=   3.9.24)119x409=

3.9.25)365x166=   3.9.26)110x627=   3.9.27)475x386=   3.9.28)768x129=

3.9.29)236x642=   3.9.30)790x543=   3.9.31)375x461=   3.9.32) 161x616=

3.9.34)793x265=   3.9.35)314x5611=   3.9.36)2664x8551=   3.9.37)21x568=

3.9.38) 571	3.9.39) 2889	3.90.40)1653	3.9.41) 781	3.9.42) 3256
x343	x566	x327	x679	x124

3.9.43) 245	3.9.44) 175	3.9.45) 267	3.9.46) 132	3.9.47) 199
x31	x46	x376	x988	x337

The following table details the number of cookies baked on each pan.

Number of cookie pans	Number of cookies
2	12
3	18
4	
6	36
8	48

3.9.w1) How many cookies where baked on 4 pans?

3.9.w2) How many cookies on 7 pans?

3.9.w3) How many cookies on each pan?

3.9.w4) Brad put four turtles in each pond. He has 6 ponds. How many turtle does he have?

3.9.w5) Elizabeth gave 6 rhinos 7 carrots each, how many carrots did she give the rhinos?

For one on one tutoring via skype at $35.00/Hr.; contact me at marksmathtutoring@yahoo.com

3.9.w6) There are four pairs of socks in each package. Which table below shows the relationship between the number of socks and the number of packages.

a)

Number of Packages	4	5	6	8
Number of Socks	12	15	18	21

b)

Number of Packages	4	5	6	8
Number of Socks	16	18	20	22

c)

Number of Packages	4	5	6	8
Number of Socks	16	20	24	32

d)

Number of Packages	4	5	6	8
Number of Socks	1	13	24	35

3.9.w7) There are two different types of cupcakes for sale
      # 5 boxes with 6 chocolate cupcakes in each
      # there are 42 vanilla cupcakes on the table
What is the total number of cupcakes on sale?

3.9.w8) What number goes in the box to make the mathematical statement true $\bigcirc \times 6 = 42$

3.9.w9) The baseball team bought 7 boxes of candy bars to sell. Each box has 9 candy bars in them. How many bars do they have to sell?

3.9.w10) In the equations below, the Δ always represents the same number.
    $\square + \Delta = 8$
    $\Delta \times \Delta = 4$
    What is the value of $\square$?

3.9.w11) The following table describes the number of potatoes in a bag.

Number of bags	1	4	6	7
Number of Potatoes	15	60		105

Each bag has the same number of potatoes in it. How many potatoes are in 6 bags?
a) 45, because 105-60=45
b) 90, because 6X15=90
c) 45, because 60-15=45
d) 75, because 15+60=75

3.9.w12) At the bakery the cupcakes are in boxes with 12 cupcakes each. If you count in groups of 12 which numbers will you use?
    a) 12, 24, 38, 42
    b) 10, 20, 30, 40
    c) 12, 24, 36, 48
    d) 36, 48, 59, 61

3.9.W13) The table below show the total number of horses for different number of stalls

Number of stalls	1	3	5	7
Number of Horses	5	15		35

    There is a equal number of horses in each stall. Which equation is the best way to determine the number if horses in 5 stalls?
    a) 3+15=, b) 5X15=, c) 5+15=, d) 5X5=

3.9.w14) You made cupcakes for your school and put them in 8 boxes. There are 73 cupcakes in each box. How many cupcakes did you make.

3.9.w15) The table below show the total number of apples in different number of bags

Number of bags	1	2	3	5
Number of apples	12	24		60

There is a equal number of apples in each bag. How many apples are in 3 bags?

3.9.w16) The school sells 96 cookies every day. How many cookies will they sell in 8 days?

3.9.w17) There are 28 apple pies, and 17 peach pies. Each is for sale for $7.00. How much money will it take to buy all of the pies?

3.9.w18) The table below lists the number of rabbits in different number of cages.

Number of cages	Number of rabbits
3	12
5	20
7	28
8	
10	40

Each cage contains the same number of rabbits. What is one way to determine the number of rabbits in 8 cages
    a) find the difference between 40 and 28
    b) find the product of 8X4
    c) find the sum of 40 and 28
    d)find the difference between 40 and 10.

3.9.w19) The table below shows the number of people that enter a public bus each hour.

Number of hours	Number of people
1	16
2	32
4	
5	80
8	128

Each hour the same number of people enter the bus. How many people entered the bus in 5 hours?
a) 48, because 128-80=48
b) 64, because 4X16=64
c) 48, because 32+16=48
d) 16, because 32÷16=2

3.9.w20) While on a field trip to the ocean, 5 kids collect 15 shells each, which expression can be used to determine the total number of shells collected?
    a) 15÷5=
    b) 15X5=
    c) 15+5=
    d) 15-5=

Croquis of a Deliberate Crime

YouTube

3.9.w21) The table below shows the total number of kids in different number of buses.

Number of buses	Number of Kids
2	24
5	60
6	
7	84
9	108

Each bus has the same number of kids in it. How many kids total will be in 6 buses?

3.9.w22) Andy practices math 2 hours a day. How many hours will he practice in 9 days?

3.9.w23) Michelle practices math 3 hours a day, and history 2 hours a day. What is the total number of hours in 7 days she practices?

3.9.w24) Emery drew 6 rows of dogs. Each row has 8 dogs in it. How many dogs did she draw?

3.9.w25) The table below shows the number of dogs of different colors.

Color of Dog	Number of Dogs
Black	48
Yellow	32
Brown	24
Spotted	56

The picture graph below represents the same information

Color of Dogs	Number of Dogs
Black	X X X X X X
Yellow	X X X X
Brown	X X X
Spotted	X X X X X X X

Which Key completes the picture graph?
a) Each X means 6 dogs
b) Each X means 8 dogs
c) Each X means 4 dogs
d) Each X means 2 dogs.

3.9.w26) John has 16 packages a baseball cards. Each pack has 6 cards in it. He gives 12 to a friend. Which mathematical statement below will help determine the amount of cards he has left?
a) 16x12-6=186
b) 16x6-12=84
c) 12+6+16=34
d) 12X6-16=56

Croquis of a
Deliberate
Crime

YouTube

3.9.w27) I eat 4 apple a day. Which table below describes the number of apples total I have eaten in 4, 6, 7 days

A)

NUMBER OF DAYS	TOTAL NUMBER OF APPLES
4	16
6	24
7	28

C)

NUMBER OF DAYS	TOTAL NUMBER OF APPLES
4	16
6	22
7	28

B)

NUMBER OF DAYS	TOTAL NUMBER OF APPLES
4	16
6	24
7	26

D)

NUMBER OF DAYS	TOTAL NUMBER OF APPLES
4	18
6	24
7	28

3.9.w28) If a restaurant charges $6.00 per meal which table below describes the cost for a specific number of meals

A)

Number of Meals	4	5	7	9
Total Cost of Meals	$24	$30	$44	$54

C)

Number of Meals	4	5	7	9
Total Cost of Meals	$24	$30	$42	$54

B)

Number of Meals	4	5	7	9
Total Cost of Meals	$24	$28	$42	$48

D)

Number of Meals	4	5	7	9
Total Cost of Meals	$26	$28	$42	$52

3.9.w29) I sold pies at a rate of $7.00 per pie. Which tables below show this relationship?

A)

NUMBER OF PIES	TOTAL COST
2	$14
4	$26
6	$42
7	$49
8	$56

C)

NUMBER OF PIES	TOTAL COST
2	$14
4	$28
6	$42
7	$49
8	$56

B)

NUMBER OF PIES	TOTAL COST
2	$14
4	$28
6	$42
7	$48
8	$56

D)

NUMBER OF PIES	TOTAL COST
2	$14
4	$32
6	$42
7	$48
8	$56

3.9.w31) Given the mathematical statement below.

◇ X 10 = ○

Which table below represents this relationship

a)

◇	○
26	36
34	44
57	67
69	79

c)

◇	○
26	260
34	340
57	570
69	690

b)

◇	○
26	27
34	35
57	58
69	70

d)

◇	○
26	2.6
34	3.4
57	5.7
69	6.9

3.9.w32) Your soccer team plays 16 games a year. How many games will they play in 24 years?

3.9.w33) Each box has 16 rocks in it. If there are 37 boxes how many rocks total are there?

3.9.w34) If you sell boxes of cookies. The table below shows the number of cookies in each box.

BOXES	27	35	69	121
COOKIES	2,700	3,500		12,100

How many cookies will be in 69 boxes?

3.9.w35) If you mow 6 lawns a day, 7 days a week for 8 weeks and earn $12.00 per lawn how much money have you earned?

3.9.w36) Given the numerical sequence shown below
18, 21, 24, 27
Which of the tables below shows this relationship

a)

NUMBER	RELATIONSHIP	ANSWER
17	17+1	18
20	20+1	21
23	23+1	24
26	26+1	27

c)

NUMBER	RELATIONSHIP	ANSWER
18	18+0	18
21	21+0	21
24	24+0	24
27	27+0	27

b)

NUMBER	RELATIONSHIP	ANSWER
6	6X3=	18
7	7X3=	21
8	8X3=	24
9	9X3=	27

d)

NUMBER	RELATIONSHIP	ANSWER
18	18X1=	18
21	21X1=	21
24	24X1=	24
27	27X1=	27

3.9.w37) There are 36 kids in a class rooom. There are 25 class rooms. How many kids in this school?

3.9.w38) If I put 100 cupcakes in each box and there are 48 boxes, how many cupcakes do I have?

3.9.w39) Given the numerical relationship shown below

$$\diamondsuit \times 15 = \bigcirc$$

Which table below best describes this relationship.

a)

$\diamondsuit$	2	4	6	8
$\bigcirc$	17	19	21	23

c)

$\diamondsuit$	2	4	6	8
$\bigcirc$	13	11	9	7

b)

$\diamondsuit$	2	4	6	8
$\bigcirc$	15	30	45	60

d)

$\diamondsuit$	2	4	6	8
$\bigcirc$	30	60	90	120

3.9.w41) The following table shows the number of apples in each pie.

NUMBER OF PIES	NUMBER OF APPLES
1	32
2	64
3	96
4	128

Which of the following equations best described this relationship
a) total number of pies + 31 = total number of apples
b) total number of pies X 32 = total number of apples
c) total number of pies ÷ 31 = total number of apples
d) total number of pies - 31 = total number of apples

3.9.w42) If I throw the ball for my dog 34 times a day for 56 days. How many times have I thrown the ball for him?

3.9.w43) A season pass for the movie theater cost $100. If 125 people buy one how much money did the theater make?

3.9.w44) There are 49 boxes of light bulbs. Each box has 24 bulbs in it. What is the total number of light bulbs?

3.9.w45) If I buy 6 boxes of cookies and each has 8 cookies in it. What is the total number of cookies I have bought?

3.9.w46) I put the same number of chocolate chips in each cookie, and the relationship describing how many each cookie gets is described in the table below.

NUMBER OF COOKIES	20	25	30	35
NUMBER OF CHIPS	300	375	450	525

Which of the following equations below describes this relationship?
a) Number of Cookies + 250 = Number of Chips
b) Number of Cookies - 250 = Number of Chips
c) Number of Cookies X 15 = Number of Chips
d) Number of Cookies ÷ 15 = Number of Chips

3.9.w48) There are 420 tress in a orchards. Which of the following equations can describe the shape of the orchard?
a) 7 rows of 70 tress = 420
b) 6 rows of 70 tress = 420
c) 8 rows of 54 tress = 420
d) 9 rows of 50 trees = 420

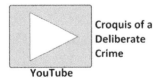

Croquis of a
Deliberate
Crime

YouTube

3.10 Division-no remainders

3.10.1) 2÷1=   3.10.2) 2÷2=   3.10.3) 3÷1=   3.10.4) 3÷3=   3.10.5) 4÷1=   3.10.6) 4÷2=

3.10.7) 4÷4=   3.10.8) 5÷1=   3.10.9) 5÷5=   3.10.10) 6÷1=   3.10.11) 6÷2=   3.10.12) 6÷3=

3.10.13) 6÷6=   3.10.14) 7÷1=   3.10.15) 7÷7=   3.10.16) 8÷1=   3.10.17) 8÷2=   3.10.18) 8÷4=

3.10.19) 8÷8=   3.10.20) 9÷1=   3.10.21) 9÷3=   3.10.22) 9÷9=   3.10.23) 10÷1=   3.10.24) 10÷2=

3.10.25) 10/5=   3.10.26) 10/10=   3.10.27) 12/1=   3.10.28) 12/2=   3.10.29) 12/3=   3.10.30) 12/4=

3.10.31) 12/6=   3.10.32) 12/12=   3.10.33) 14/1=   3.10.34) 14/2=   3.10.35) 14/7=   3.10.36) 14/14=

3.10.37) 15/1=   3.10.38) 15/3=   3.10.39) 15/5=   3.10.40) 15/15=   3.10.41) 18/3=   3.10.42) 18/6=

3.10.43) 20   3.10.44) 9   3.10.45) 6   3.10.46) 15   3.10.47) 8   3.10.48) 10
         ÷2   ÷3   ÷2   ÷5   ÷4   ÷2

3.10.49) 8   3.10.50) 8   3.10.51) 6   3.10.52) 7   3.10.53) 8   3.10.54) 2
         ÷8   ÷2   ÷3   ÷7   ÷2   ÷2

The picture blow shows how many flowers Sarah bought to put in her garden.

She will plant them in rows of 8 flowers.

3.10.w1) How many rows will she have once completed?

3.10.w2) How many rows will have 4 flowers?

3.10.w3)How many flowers are not in a row of 4 flowers?

3.10.w4) Mike has 15 tomatoes to but on 5 hamburgers. He wants to deposit the same amount of tomatoes on each burger. How many does each hamburger get?

3.10.w5) Mrs. Garcia has 42 cups. She wants to put them in 6 boxes each with the same amount of cups. How many cups does each box have?

3.10.w6) Aaron will place 45 rocks from his collection on a self. Each shelf will have 9 rocks. How many selves does he need?

3.10.w7) 6 students from your school go to the zoo with 11 carrots each. They want to feed 3 animals with equal number of carrots. Which equation is the best way to figure out how many carrots each animal will get.
a) 6X11÷3= b) 6X2÷11=, c) 2X11÷6=, d) 2X11X6=

3.10.w8) The bicycle shop has 42 bike for sale. They are arranged into 6 rows with an even number of bikes in each row. How many bikes are there in each row?

3.10.w9) The picture bellows shows the number of bike at a store.

The bike will be arranged in three rows with the same number in each. Which expression below will determine the number of bikes in each row.
a) 6, because 18÷3=6, b) 8, because 15÷3+3=8, c) 5, because 15÷3=5, d) 3, because 15÷5=3

3.10.w10) The band director has 28 trumpets

He will put a same number of trumpets on 7 selves. How many trumpets will be on each self?
a) 8, because 28÷7=8
b) 4, because 28÷7=4
c) 7, because 28÷4=7
d) 4, because 28÷7=7

3.10.w11) The candle shown below will be arranged in 4 rows.

Each row will have the same number of candles. Which mathematical express is best for determining the number of candles in each row?
a) 20÷4=5
b) 10÷5=2
c) 20÷5=4
d) 10÷2=5

Croquis of a
Deliberate
Crime
YouTube

If you don't get the correct answer, and want an explanation on how to work the problem, go to YouTube and type in "MMT" then the problem number. An example would be, MMT 3.9.w12,. The video will show you how to work problem 3.9.w12.

For one on one tutoring via skype at $35.00/Hr.; contact me at marksmathtutoring@yahoo.com

3.11.W12) Nellie is putting on a dog show in her neighborhood. There are 16 dogs entered as shown below.

If she puts the dogs into 4 rows, Each row has the same number of dogs. How many dogs will be in each row?
a) 12, 16÷4=12
b) 4, 16÷4=4
c) 3, 6÷3=2
d) 8, 16÷2=8

3.10.w13) Verna bought 20 trees for his farm, as shown below.

He wants to plant them in 5 rows. Each row will have the same number of trees in it. Which mathematical expression will help in determining the number of trees in each row?
a) 20X4=100
b) 4X6=24
c) 20÷5=4
d) 20÷2=10

3.10.w14) Danielle sorted 40 greeting cards into 5 equally sized groups. Which statement below is **NOT** in the same fact family as 40÷5=8
a) 8X5=40
b) 5X4=8
c) 40÷8=5
d) 5X8=40

Croquis of a
Deliberate
Crime

YouTube

If you don't get the correct answer, and want an explanation on how to work the problem, go to YouTube and type in "MMT" then the problem number. An example would be, MMT 3.9.w12,. The video will show you how to work problem 3.9.w12.

For one on one tutoring via skype at $35.00/Hr.; contact me at marksmathtutoring@yahoo.com

3.10.w15) John has 14 model boat to play with, as shown below.

While playing with them in the bath, he arranges them in 2 rows with equal number in each. Which statement below will help determine the number of boats in each row?
a) 14÷2=7
b) 2X14=28
c) 14-2=10
d) 14÷7=2

3.11 Inequalities
State if these are true or false
3.11.1) 3<1   3.11.2) 5>5   3.11.3) 7$\leq$7   3.11.4) 14<7   3.11.5) 56<81   3.11.6) 4>8
3.11.7) 81<45   3.11.8) 85$\geq$51   3.11.9) 3<9   3.11.10) 43>67 3.11.11) 2<8   3.11.12) 41<41
3.11.13) 76$\leq$76 3.11.14) 78<98   3.11.15) 8<4   3.11.16) 9$\leq$12   3.11.17) 76$\leq$67 3.11.18) 543>73
3.11.19) 0<1   3.11.20) 13<7   3.11.21) 67>43 3.11.22) 13$\geq$31 3.11.23)45<45   3.11.24) 123>237

3.11.w1) A group of number is shown below

| 2467 | 2586 | 2775 | 2911 |

Which statement below is true:
a) 2586 >2476 because the 5>4.
b) 2467>2911 because 67>11
c) 2775>2467 because 75 is greater than 67
d) 2467<2586 because 67<86

3.11.w2) A groups of number is shown below

| 137 | 366 | 415 | 110 |

Which statement below is true
a) 415<366 because 66<15
b) 137>415 because 37 is greater than 15
c) 366>415 because 6>5
d) 110<366 because 1<3

For one on one tutoring via skype at $35.00/Hr.; contact me at marksmathtutoring@yahoo.com

3.11.w3) A group of numbers is shown below

| 4 | 8 | 9 | 5 |

Which statement below is **NOT** true
a) 4<8
b)9>4
c) 9>8
d)4>9

3.11.w4) A group of numbers is shown below

| 827 | 199 | 1127 | 531 |

Which statement below is true
a) 827>1127 because the 8 > 11
b) 199>531 because 1>5
c) 531>1127 because 53>11
d) 1127>827 because 1>0

3.11.w5) The following list shows three clues about a number I am thinking about.
the number is greater than 3578
the number is less than 5587
There is a 6 in the hundreds place
Which of the following could be this number
a) 6156
b) 4729
c) 4699
d)2687

3.11.w6) The following list shows three clues about a number I am thinking about.
the number is greater than 379
the number is less than 421
There is a 8 in the tens place
Which of the following could be this number
a) 581
b) 381
c) 289
d)417

Croquis of a
Deliberate
Crime
YouTube

If you don't get the correct answer, and want an explanation on how to work the problem, go to YouTube and type in "MMT" then the problem number. An example would be, MMT 3.9.w12,. The video will show you how to work problem 3.9.w12.

3.11.w7) The following list shows three clues about a number I am thinking about.
the number is greater than 28
the number is less than 54
There is a 7 in the ones place
Which of the following could be this number
a) 42
b) 73
c) 47
d)31

3.11.w8) The sum of 6 thousands 4 hundreds 5 tens and 2 ones is which of the following
a) 6542
b) 2546
c)6452
d) 17

3.11.w9) The sum of 8 thousands 3 hundreds 0 tens and 1 ones is which of the following
a) 8031
b) 1038
c) 8301
d) 12

Croquis of a
Deliberate
Crime
YouTube

If you don't get the correct answer, and want an explanation on how to work the problem, go to YouTube and type in "MMT" then the problem number. An example would be, MMT 3.9.w12,. The video will show you how to work problem 3.9.w12.

For one on one tutoring via skype at $35.00/Hr.; contact me at marksmathtutoring@yahoo.com

4.0 GEOMETRY

4.1) Which of the following is not a Rhombus, trapezoid, rectangle or square?

A)   B)   C)   D)

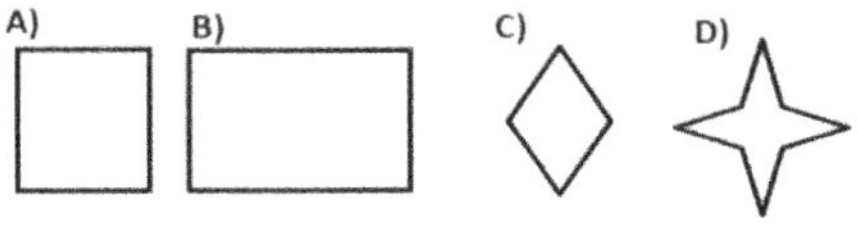

4.2) Which of the following is not a polygon?

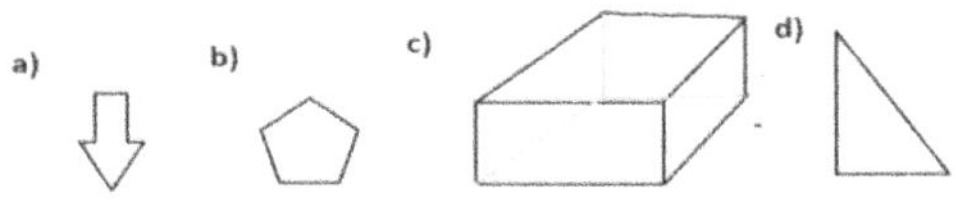

a)   b)   c)   d)

4.3) Which of the following figures is not a quadrilateral?

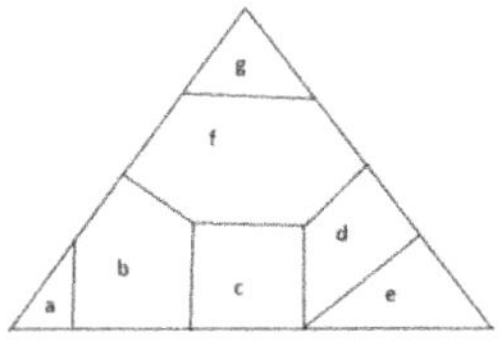

4.4) Which of the following is not a Rhombus, trapezoid, rectangle or square?

a)
b)
c)
d)

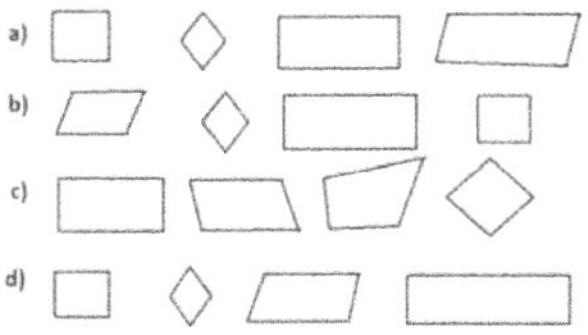

4.5) Which statement is true about the following figures?

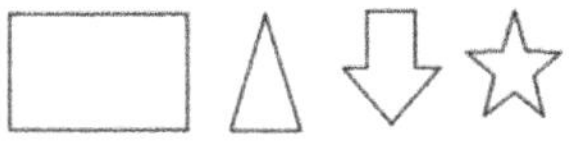

a) All the figures are Rhombuses
b) All the figures are polygons
c) All the figures are parallelograms
d) All figures are Quadrilaterals

4.61) Which of the following is required for a pentagon?
a) right angles
b) parallel lines
c) 4 vertices
d) five sides

Croquis of a Deliberate Crime

YouTube

4.62) The following figures share a common characteristic.

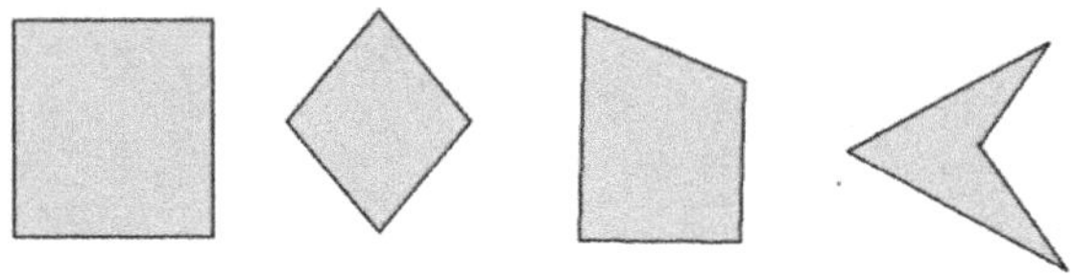

a) all are trapezoids
b) all are squares
c) all are triangles
d) all are quadrilaterals

4.39) Which of the following figure is not a pentagon

4.40) Which of the following figure is not a hexagon

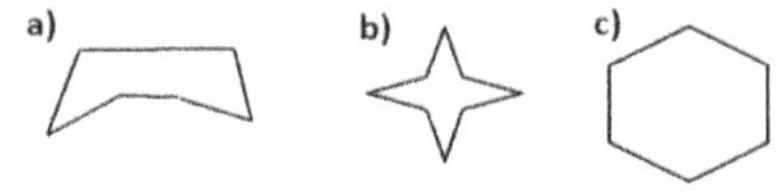

4.6) Which figure does not have symmetry

4.7) Which figure does not have symmetry

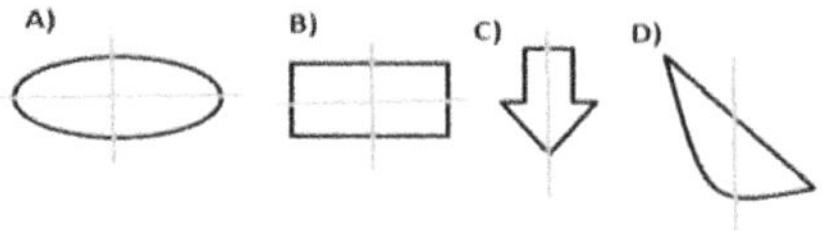

4.65) The drawing below is only half of the figure. The rest of it is a symmetry about the line AB

Which one of the following could complete this figure

a)

b)

c)

d)

4.66) Which drawing below has two lines of symmetry?

A) B) C) D)

4.67) Which of the drawings below has only one line of symmetry?

A) B) C) D)

4.68) Which of the following figures has both a horizontal and a vertical line of symmetry?

A) B) C) D)

4.69) Which figure below has only a horizontal line of symmetry?

A) B) C) D)

4.70) Which figure below does not have a vertical line of symmetry, no horizontal?

A) B) C) D)

4.8) How many edges does the figure have?

4.9) How many edges does the figure have?

4.10) How many edges does the figure have?

4.11) How many edges does the figure have?

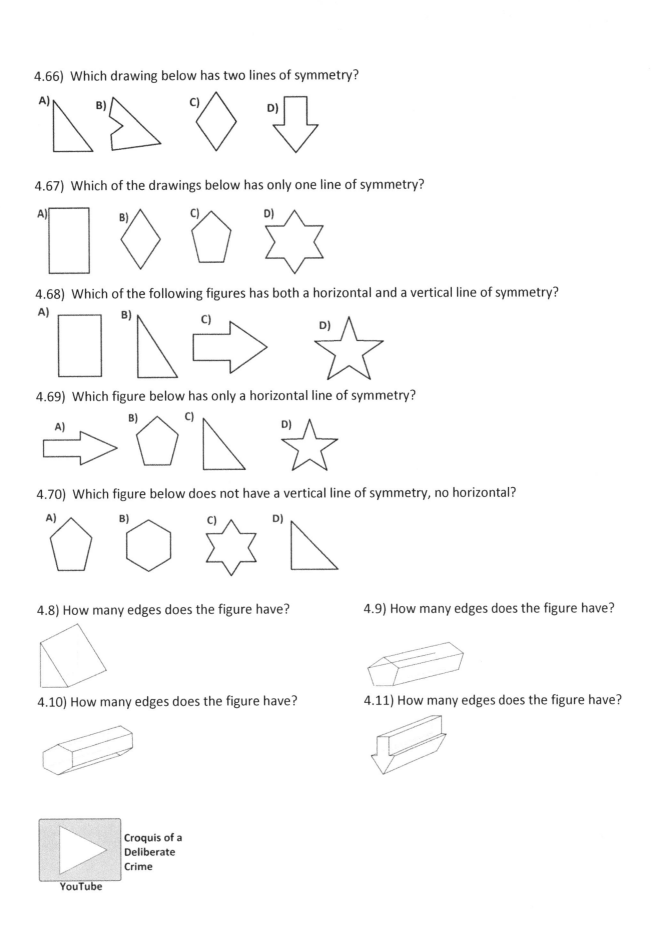

4.41) How many edges does the figure have?

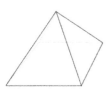

4.42) How many edges does the figure have?

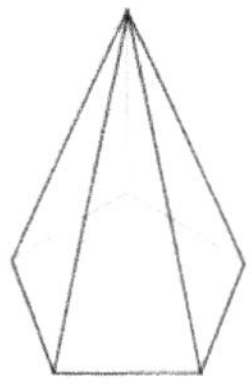

4.12) Which of the following figures is made of four congruent shapes

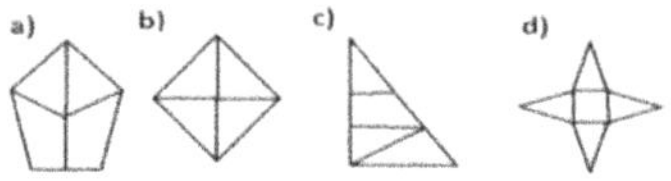

4.13) Given the figure below:

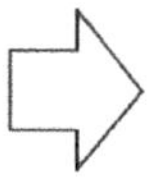

Which figure below appears to be congruent?

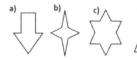

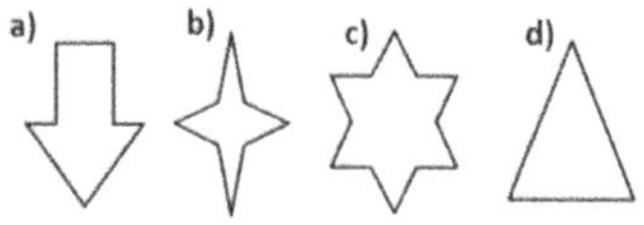

4.14) A triangle has three equal sides. If the perimeter is 18 cm how long is each side?

4.15) The following figure was created with two congruent triangle on each end of a rectangle. What is the perimeter of this shape?

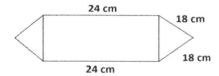

4.16) The following figure has a line of symmetry as shown. What is the perimeter of this figure?

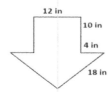

4.17) Ed needs to fence his back yard in. The dimensions of the yard are shown below

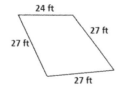

If he has 103 feet of fence does he have enough to do the job?

4.18) Given the drawings of two rectangles below

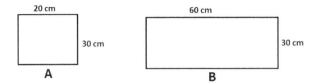

What statement below is true
a) The perimeter of A is 40 cm less than the perimeter of B
b) The perimeter of B is 40 cm less than the perimeter of A
c) The perimeter of A is 80 cm less than the perimeter of B
d) The perimeter of B is 80 cm less than the perimeter of A

4.19) The two figures below are drawn with congruent sides.

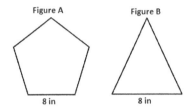

Which statement below is true
a)The perimeter of Figure A is 16 inches larger the Figure B
b)The perimeter of Figure B is 16 inches larger the Figure A
c)The perimeter of Figure A is 24 inches larger the Figure B
d)The perimeter of Figure B and A are the same

4.20) Sarah needs to fence in her garden to keep animals out. The garden has the dimensions shown below

If she has 110 feet of fence, does she have enough?

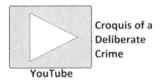

Croquis of a
Deliberate
Crime

YouTube

If you don't get the correct answer, and want an explanation on how to work the problem, go to YouTube and type in "MMT" then the problem number. An example would be, MMT 3.9.w12,. The video will show you how to work problem 3.9.w12.

For one on one tutoring via skype at $35.00/Hr.; contact me at marksmathtutoring@yahoo.com

4.21) Steve has a garden he needs to fence in. He has 64 feet of fence. Which in of the following figure could not be the dimensions of his garden?

a)

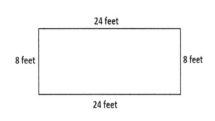

c)

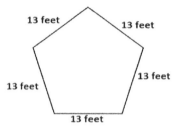

b)

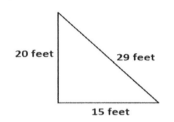

d)

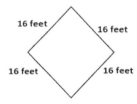

4.22) Which of the following figures does not have a perimeter of 120 cm?

a)

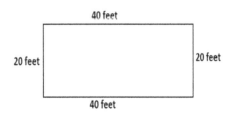

c)

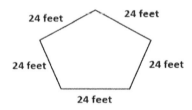

b)

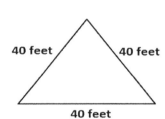

d)

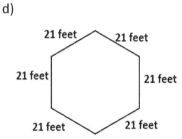

4.23) If a triangle has a perimeter of 26 inches, and two sides are 11 inches each. What is the length of the third side?

Croquis of a Deliberate Crime

YouTube

4.24) What is the area of the letter H below if each square is 1 foot square

4.25) What is the area of the letter L below if each square is 1 foot square

4.26) What is the difference between the area of the letter O and the letter T shown below if each square is I Meter squared

 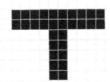

4.27) Which equation below best describes the mathematical equation to determine the area of the shaded box below?

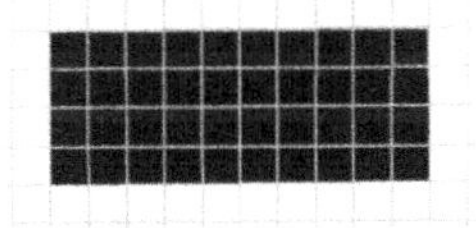

a) 6-4=2
b) 10X4=40
c) 24÷4=6
d) 6+4=10

4.28) I started to tie my kitchen floor as shown in the diagram below. Each small square is 1 foot square.

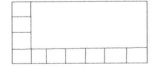

Once finished tiling the floor how many ties will be used?

Croquis of a
Deliberate
Crime

YouTube

4.29) Given the diagram below what is the area of the rectangle?

4.30) Which of the following rectangles has an area of 42?

a)

c)

b)

d)

4.31) If your floor measures 9 feet by 17 feet, what is the area of this floor in feet square?

4.32) If a garden has the shape of the drawing below and each square is 1 meter square, what is the area of the garden?

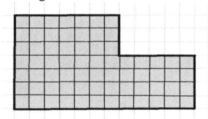

 Croquis of a Deliberate Crime

YouTube

If you don't get the correct answer, and want an explanation on how to work the problem, go to YouTube and type in "MMT" then the problem number. An example would be, MMT 3.9.w12,. The video will show you how to work problem 3.9.w12.

For one on one tutoring via skype at $35.00/Hr.; contact me at marksmathtutoring@yahoo.com

4.33) Which statement below is true about the two figures below

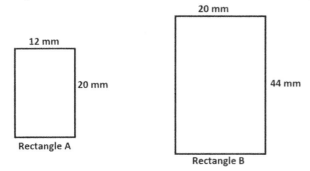

a) The perimeter rectangle A is 56 mm small than rectangle B
b) The perimeter rectangle A is 64 mm small than rectangle B
c) The perimeter rectangle A is 32 mm small than rectangle B
d) The perimeter rectangle A is 8 mm small than rectangle B

4.55) What is the perimeter of a rectangular poster with one side 18 inches and the other 8 inches.

4.56) If your garden is square with sides 39 feet, what is the perimeter?

Croquis of a
Deliberate
Crime

If you don't get the correct answer, and want an explanation on how to work the problem, go to YouTube and type in "MMT" then the problem number. An example would be, MMT 3.9.w12,. The video will show you how to work problem 3.9.w12.

For one on one tutoring via skype at $35.00/Hr.; contact me at marksmathtutoring@yahoo.com

5 FRACTIONS

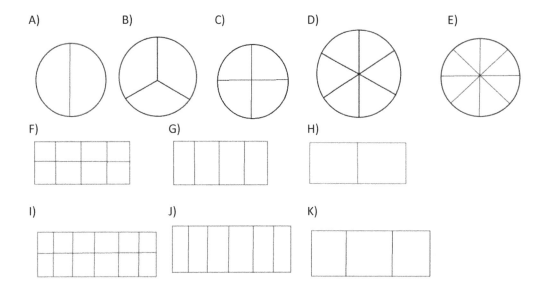

A)   B)   C)   D)   E)

F)   G)   H)

I)   J)   K)

For the following problems redraw each figure before shading in the parts. This way you can reuse them.

5.1) for figure A) color ½ of the circle

5.2) for figure B) color 2/3 of the circle

5.3) for figure I) color 7/12 of the square

5.4) for figure J) color 5/6 of the square

5.5) for figure F) color 5/8 of the square

5.6) for figure E) color 5/8 of the circle

5.7) color 2/4 of figure C) and 1/2 of Figure A) Are they the same?

5.8) color 3/4 of figure C) and 6/8 of Figure E) Are they the same?

5.9) color 2/3 of figure B) and 3/6 of Figure D) Are they the same?

5.10) color 2/8 of figure E) and 1/4 of Figure C) Are they the same?

5.11) color 2/4 of figure G) and 2/8 of Figure F) Are they the same?

5.12) color 6/12 of figure I) and 3/4 of Figure G) Are they the same?

5.13) color 2/3 of figure K) and 4/6 of Figure J) Are they the same?

5.14) color 2/4 of figure C) and 3/8 of Figure E) Are they the same? If not which one is greater?

5.15) color 2/3 of figure B) and 3/6 of Figure D) Are they the same? If not which one is less?

5.16) color 3/8 of figure E) and 3/4 of Figure C) Are they the same? If not which one is less?

5.17) color 1/3 of figure B) and 3/8 of Figure E) Are they the same? If not which one is greater?

5.18) color 3/4 of figure G) and 1/2 of Figure H) Are they the same? If not which one is greater?

5.19) color 1/3 of figure K) and 1/3 of Figure J) Are they the same? If not which one is less?

5.20) color 4/12 of figure I) and 1/3 of Figure K) Are they the same? If not which one is greater?

5.21) color 2/12 of figure I) and 2/6 of Figure J) Are they the same? If not which one is greater?

5.22) color 2/6 of figure J) and 2/3 of Figure K) Are they the same? If not which one is greater?

5.23) color 2/4 of figure G) and 4/8 of Figure F) Are they the same? If not which one is greater?

5.24) color 4/6 of figure J) and 1/2 of Figure H) Are they the same? If not which one is less?

5.25) color 6/12 of figure I) and 3/6 of Figure J) Are they the same? If not which one is less?

5.27) color 2/12 of figure I) and 2/6 of Figure J) Are they the same? If not which one is greater?

5.28) color 1/3 of figure K) and 2/6 of Figure J) Are they the same? If not which one is less?

5.29) color 1/8 of figure F) and 1/4 of Figure G) Are they the same? If not which one is greater?

5.30) Sarah shaded the following figure

Which fraction best reprsents the shaded area
a) 2/3, b) 3/4, c) 1/2, d) 4/4

5.31) Edward shaded the following figure

Which fraction best represents the shaded area
a) 1/4, b) 3/2, c) 2/3, d) 1/3

5.32) Mike saded th following figure

Which fraction best represents the saded area
a) 1/8, b) 1/4, c) 1/2, d) 7/8

5.33) Jonny shaded the following figure

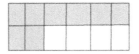

Which fraction best represents the saded area
a) 5/8, b) 8/12, c) 2/3, d) 3/4

5.34) Lynne saded the following figure

Which fraction best represents the shaded area
a) 4/6, b) 3/4, c) 2/3, d) 3/5

5.35) Lynne saded the following figure

Which fraction best represents the shaded area
a) 7/8, b) 1/8, c) 3/4, d) 5/8

5.36) Sarah ate 1/3 of a cake and her brother ate 1/4 of a pie. Which one ate the most cake?
5.37) If one apple is 3/4 of a pound and the other is 3/5 of a pound. Which apple is bigger?
5.38) If I buy 2/5 of a pound of sugar and you buy 2/3 of a pound of sugar, who bought the most?
5.39) If Al pays 3/4 of a dollar and Sue pays 3/5 of a dollar who pays the most?
5.40) Which number is smaller 1/2 or 1/3?
5.41) Which number is larger 2/3 or 2/5?
5.42) which number is larger 3/5 or 3/8?
5.43) Which number is smaller 5/8 or 5/9

5.44) Which fraction is larger 2/5 or 3/5?
5.45) which fraction is larger 1/3 or 2/3?
5.46) Which fraction is smaller 3/8 or 6/8?
5.47) which fraction is smaller 5/6 or 3/6?

Croquis of a
Deliberate
Crime

YouTube

If you don't get the correct answer, and want an explanation on how to work the problem, go to YouTube and type in "MMT" then the problem number. An example would be, MMT 3.9.w12,. The video will show you how to work problem 3.9.w12.

5.48) Verna shaded the following two figures

Which statements best describes the shaded areas
a) 7/8<5/8
b) 3/4>5/8
c)3/4>7/8
d) 7/8>5/8

5.49) Verna shaded the following two figures

 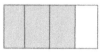

Which statements best describes the shaded areas
a) 3/4>1/4
b) 1/4>3/4
c) 1/2<1/4
d) 1/4<3/4

5.50) the following shapes are shaded as shown.

Which stament below best describes this shading
a)5/6>4/6, b) 2/6>3/6, c) 3/4< 2/3, d) 5/6=4/6

5.51) the following shapes are shaded as shown.

Which stament below best describes this shading
a)5/6>4/6, b) 3/8>3/6, c) 10/12< 3/12, d)10/12>3/12

5.52) the following shapes are shaded as shown.

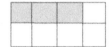 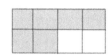

Which stament below best describes this shading
a)3/8>6/8, b) 3/8<6/8, c) 2/4< 2/8, d) 5/6<4/6

5.53) the following shapes are shaded as shown.

Which stament below best describes this shading
a)2/3>1/3, b) 2/3<1/3, c) 1/4>2/6, d) 4/6<2/6

5.54) Which statement is true
    a) 1/8<1/5<1/4<1/3, b) 1/3<1/4<1/6<1/9, c) 2/5<2/4<2/6<2/8, d) 3/5>3/7>3/8>3/2
5.55) Which statement is true
    a) 3/5<3/4<3/2<3/7, b) 3/4>3/5>3/7>3/8, c) 4/5<4/6<4/7<4/9, d) 4/5>4/6>4/3>4/8
5.56) Which statement is true
    a) 5/7>5/8>5/4>5/6, b) 4/5>4/6>4/7>4/9, c) 3/5<3/4<3/7<3/9 d) 6/7<6/4<6/5<6/9
5.57) Which statement is true
    a) 2/3<3/3<4/3<5/3, b) 3/9>5/9>6/9<1/9, c) 6/7>5/7>7/7>3/7, d) 5/6>5/4>5/3>5/2
5.58) Which statement is true
    a) 5/8<7<8<3/8<6/8, b) 3/7<9/7<6/7<8/7, c) 7/8>6/8>5/8>3/8, d) 12/4<3/4<6/4<3/4

Using <, >, ≤, ≥ to complete the following statements
5.6.66) 35, 51   5.6.67) 21, 68   5.6.68) 13, 54   5.6.69) 65, 89
5.6.70) 135, 21   5.6.71) 2134, 321   5.6.72) 12, 138   5.6.73) 789, 46
5.6.74) 533, 267   5.6.75) 887, 4567   5.6.76) 12, 476   5.6.77) 12.1, 33.7
5.6.78) 34, 34.2   5.6.79) 67.01, 67.1   5.6.80) 889.25, 889.2 5.6.81) 12.01, 13.01
5.6.82) 128.3, 128.03 5.6.83) 1.225, 1.252 5.6.84) 3.1, 4.5   5.6.85) 56.7, 65.7

 Croquis of a Deliberate Crime

YouTube

5.59) The diagram below show the amount of money I found in the street today.

How much money is this
a) $1^{\underline{51}}$
b) $1^{\underline{96}}$
c) $1^{\underline{47}}$
d) $1^{\underline{37}}$

5.60) I want to buy a candy bar. It cost $1^{\underline{86}}$. If the diagram below shows how much money I have in my pocket do I have enough money?

5.61) Is the amount of money shown below more than $0^{\underline{87}}$?

Croquis of a
Deliberate
Crime

YouTube

If you don't get the correct answer, and want an explanation on how to work the problem, go to YouTube and type in "MMT" then the problem number. An example would be, MMT 3.9.w12,. The video will show you how to work problem 3.9.w12.

For one on one tutoring via skype at $35.00/Hr.; contact me at marksmathtutoring@yahoo.com

6.0 GRAPHING

6.1) The graph below shows the number of cookies your brother ate.

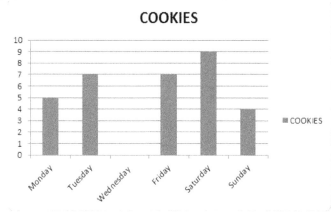

If the total of cookies eaten was 36, how many cookies were eaten on Wednesday?

6.2) What is the total weight of all the dogs shown in the graph below?

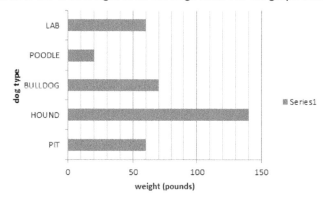

Croquis of a
Deliberate
Crime

YouTube

\# If you don't get the correct answer, and want an explanation on how to work the problem, go to YouTube and type in "MMT" then the problem number. An example would be, MMT 3.9.w12,. The video will show you how to work problem 3.9.w12.

\# For one on one tutoring via skype at $35.00/Hr.; contact me at marksmathtutoring@yahoo.com

6.3) Given the graph below

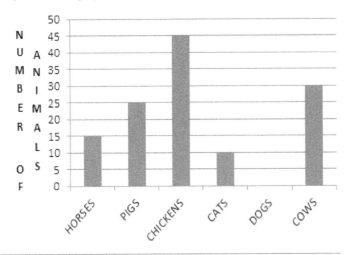

If there are 140 animals total on this farm which graph below indicated the number of cats

a)   b)   c)   d)

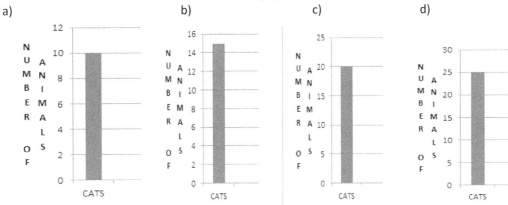

6.4) The following table describes the number of fruit trees on a farm

Type of fruit tree	Number of trees
Apple	11,256
Pear	8,765
Plum	12,367
Cherry	10,018
Peach	9,672

Which stamen is not true based on the data in the above table
a)Apples>Pear, b) Plums>Cherry, c) Peach<Cherry, d) Plum<Apple

Croquis of a
Deliberate
Crime

YouTube

If you don't get the correct answer, and want an explanation on how to work the problem, go to YouTube and type in "MMT" then the problem number. An example would be, MMT 3.9.w12,. The video will show you how to work problem 3.9.w12.

For one on one tutoring via skype at $35.00/Hr.; contact me at marksmathtutoring@yahoo.com

6.5) The graph below indicates the number of cars of each type for sale at a lot.

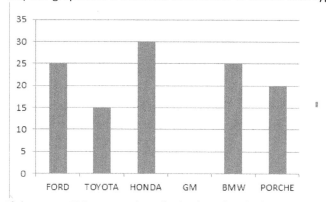

If there are 135 cars total on the lot for sale which graph below shows the number of GMs

a) b) c) d)

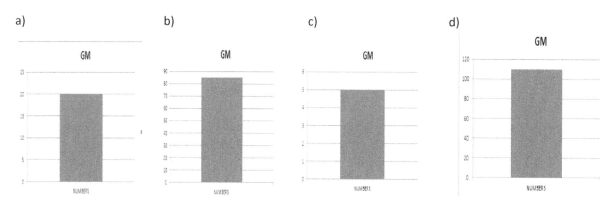

6.6) The graph below shows the number of tons of garbage collected by the city per month

	X			
	X		X	
X	X		X	X
X	X	X	X	X
X	X	X	X	X
May	June	July	Aug	May

Each **X** represented 500 pounds

Based on the graph above how many more pounds of garbage did the city collect in August than May?

6.7) The table below details the number of games for each sport

SPORT	NUMBER
SOCCER	35
FOOTBALL	17
BASEBALL	176
BASKETBALL	125

Based on the information in the table organize the sports from high to low

a) baseball, soccer, basketball, football
b) baseball, basketball, soccer, football
c) football, soccer, basketball, baseball
d) basketball, baseball, football, soccer

For one on one tutoring via skype at $35.00/Hr.; contact me at marksmathtutoring@yahoo.com

6.8) The following table details the number of minutes Mike did choirs.

		X	
X		X	
X		X	
X	X	X	X
X	X	X	X
Mon.	Tues.	Wed.	Thur.

Each X represents 10 minutes of work

How many more minutes of work did Mike do on Mon compared to Thur.?

6.9) The following table describes the number of different types of fish 4 kids have in their aquariums.

AQUARIUM	GUPPIES	ANGLES
Mary	12	4
Steve	15	5
Susan	21	7
Mark	9	3

Which statement below is correct based on the information in the tables

a) There are three time the number of guppies as angles
b) There are eight more guppies than angle
c) There are three time the number of angles as guppies
d) There is no relationship in the number of guppies and angles.

6.10) The following graph describes the number of kids in each grade who bring a sandwich to school for lunch.

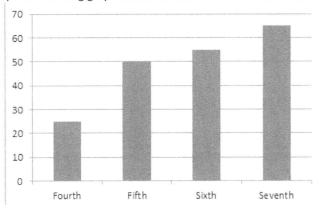

Based on the table above which statement is true

a) A total of 65 kids from the fourth and fifth grades had sandwiches
b) No grade brought 55 sandwiches
c) A total of 195 kids brought sandwiches
d) The difference between the seventh and fifth grades who brought sandwiches is 15

Croquis of a Deliberate Crime

YouTube

If you don't get the correct answer, and want an explanation on how to work the problem, go to YouTube and type in "MMT" then the problem number. An example would be, MMT 3.9.w12,. The video will show you how to work problem 3.9.w12.

6.11) The following table details the amount of a discount a store is giving based on the amount you buy.

AMOUNT OF PURCHASE	AMOUNT AFTER DISCOUNT
$23.00	$18.00
$28.00	$23.00
$33.00	$28.00
$38.00	$33.00
$43.00	$38.00

Based on the information given in the table which statement is true
a) The amount after discount minus $5.00 equals the amount of purchase
b) There is no relationship between the two values
c) The amount after discount minus $5.00 equals the amount of purchase
d) The amount after discount is always $5.00 less than the amount of purchase

6.12) The following table describes the number of kids with each name in a school

NAMES	NUMBERS
Mike	35
James	25
John	15
Elmer	40

Which table below describes this data best

A)

NAMES	NUMBERS
Mike	XXXXXXX
James	XXXXX
John	XXXX
Elmer	XXXXXXXX

Each X is equal to 5 students

C)

NAMES	NUMBERS
Mike	XXXXXX
James	XXXXX
John	XXXXX
Elmer	XXXXXXXX

Each X is equal to 5 students

B)

NAMES	NUMBERS
Mike	XXXXXXX
James	XXXXX
John	XXX
Elmer	XXXXXXXX

Each X is equal to 5 students

D)

NAMES	NUMBERS
Mike	XXXXXXXX
James	XXXXX
John	XXX
Elmer	XXXXXXX

Each X is equal to 5 students

Croquis of a Deliberate Crime

YouTube

If you don't get the correct answer, and want an explanation on how to work the problem, go to YouTube and type in "MMT" then the problem number. An example would be, MMT 3.9.w12,. The video will show you how to work problem 3.9.w12.

For one on one tutoring via skype at $35.00/Hr.; contact me at marksmathtutoring@yahoo.com

6.13) The following graph describes the number of hamburger I ate each weekday.

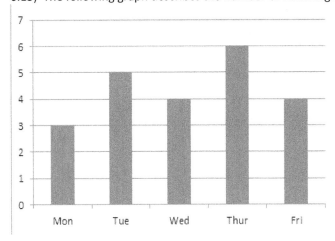

Which of the following tables best represents this data

a)

DAY	Mon	Tue	Wed	Thur	Fri
NUMBER	3	5	6	4	6

b)

DAY	Mon	Tue	Wed	Thur	Fri
NUMBER	3	6	5	7	5

c)

DAY	Mon	Tue	Wed	Thur	Fri
NUMBER	3	5	4	6	4

d)

DAY	Mon	Tue	Wed	Thur	Fri
NUMBER	3	7	4	7	5

6.14) The following table details the number of fish dinner a resturant sales

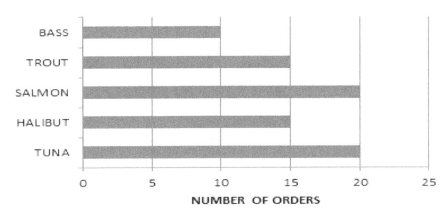

NUMBER OF ORDERS

Which of the following tables best describes the data in the graph above

A)

FISH DINNER	NUMBER
BASS	10
TROUT	20
SLAMON	15
HALIBUT	15
TUNA	20

C)

FISH DINNER	NUMBER
BASS	10
TROUT	15
SLAMON	20
HALIBUT	15
TUNA	20

B)

FISH DINNER	NUMBER
BASS	10
TROUT	15
SLAMON	20
HALIBUT	25
TUNA	20

D)

FISH DINNER	NUMBER
BASS	10
TROUT	15
SLAMON	20
HALIBUT	15
TUNA	10

6.15) The following graph details the number of books I read per year I read

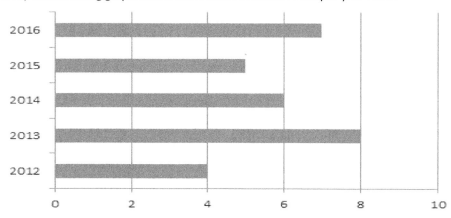

Which of the following tables best represents this data

A)

YEAR	NUMBER
2016	7
2015	5
2014	6
2013	8
2012	4

C)

YEAR	NUMBER
2016	7
2015	5
2014	8
2013	6
2012	4

B)

YEAR	NUMBER
2016	7
2015	5
2014	8
2013	8
2012	4

D)

YEAR	NUMBER
2016	7
2015	5
2014	6
2013	8
2012	6

Croquis of a
Deliberate
Crime

YouTube

If you don't get the correct answer, and want an explanation on how to work the problem, go to YouTube and type in "MMT" then the problem number. An example would be, MMT 3.9.w12,. The video will show you how to work problem 3.9.w12.

For one on one tutoring via skype at $35.00/Hr.; contact me at marksmathtutoring@yahoo.com

6.16) The following tables describes the number of times a number was picked at randon from the deck of cards

DAY OF THE WEEK	NUMBER OF TIMES
One	4
Two	6
Three	5
Four	4
Five	3
Six	2

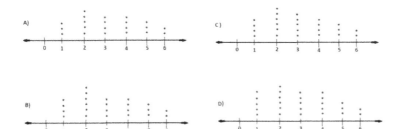

6.17) The following table details the number of miles I ran in one day

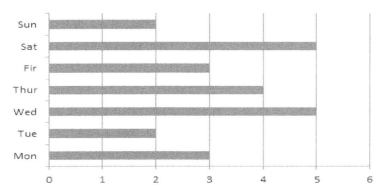

Which table below best describes this data?

A)

DAY	MILES
MON	3
TUE	2
WED	4
THUR	5
FRI	3
SAT	5
SUN	2

B)

DAY	MILES
MON	3
TUE	2
WED	5
THUR	4
FRI	3
SAT	5
SUN	3

C)

DAY	MILES
Mon	2
Tue	5
Wed	3
Thur	4
Fri	5
Sat	2
Sun	3

D)

DAY	MILES
Mon	3
Tue	2
Wed	5
Thur	4
Fri	3
Sat	5
Sun	2

6.18) The following list of numbers represents the card that was pulled from a deck.

3,2,7,6,6,7,5,10,2,3,7,3,7,1,3,

Which dot diagram below best represents this data

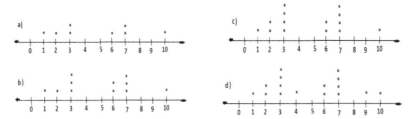

6.20) The graph below shows the number of fruits a grocery has on the shelf. Based on the this information how many more oranges than pears does the grocery have

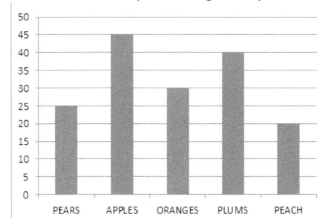

6.22) The graph below show the number of cookies I ate in each weekday.

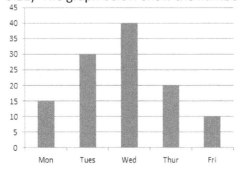

If I want to eat the same number of cookies each day how many more should I eat on Tues to equal the number I ate on Wed?

Croquis of a Deliberate Crime

YouTube

6.24) The following graph shows the number of fish I caught each day during the summer.

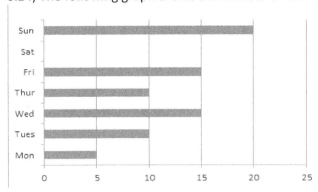

If I caught a total of 85 fish, how many must I have caught on Sat?

6.25) The following is a list of the length in inches of the fish I caught this summer.
          12,14,16,12,18,22,16,24,16,18,13,23
Which of the table below best represents this data

a)

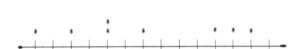

c)

STEAM	LEAF
1	2,2,3,4,6,6,6,8,8
2	2,3,4

b)

d)

steam	leaf
1	2, 4, 6, 8
2	2, 3, 4
3	0

6.26) The following table list the amount of fruit a farmer produced last year

FRUIT TYPE	NUMBER
Apples	125,835,266
Pears	217,346,893
Oranges	187,663,524
Peaches	237,894,332
Plums	109,475,872

Based on the information in this table which list below organizes this data from lowest to highest.
a) Plums, Oranges, Apples, Pears, Peaches
b) Plums, Apples, Oranges, Pears, Peaches
c) Peaches, Pears, Oranges, Apples, Plums
d) Plums, Apples, Oranges, Peaches, Pears

6.27) The following table list the number of fish I caught this summer based on their type.

FISH TYPE	NUMBER
Bass	45
Trout	
Salmon	17

If I caught a total of 63 fish how many Trout must I have caught?

6.30) Given the information in the table below

WEIGHT	½	1	1 ½	2	2 ½	3	3 ½	4
NUMBER	2	4	0	3	6	2	1	4

a)

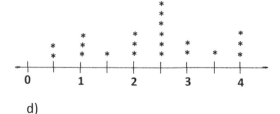

b)

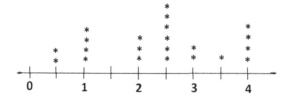

c)

d)

If you don't get the correct answer, and want an explanation on how to work the problem, go to YouTube and type in "MMT" then the problem number. An example would be, MMT 3.9.w12,. The video will show you how to work problem 3.9.w12.

For one on one tutoring via skype at $35.00/Hr.; contact me at marksmathtutoring@yahoo.com

7.0 MEASURMENTS

7.1) Use a ruler to measure in centimeters the two arrows below. What is the difference in their heights

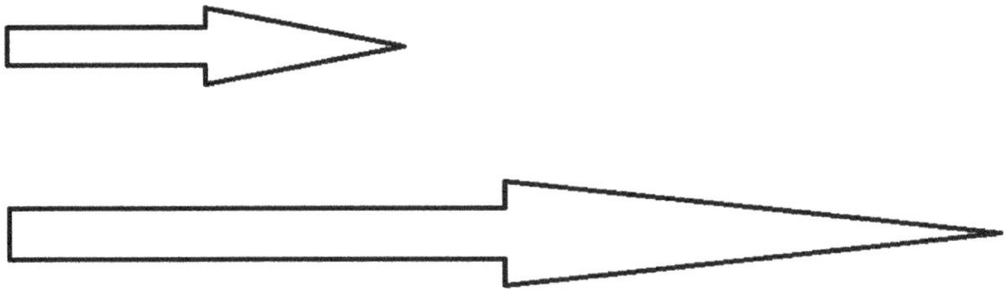

7.2) Use a ruler to measure and determine the perimeter, to 1/2 of an inch, of the following drawing

7.3) Use a ruler to determine the length to the nearest ½ inch of the following lines

A) ———————————————

B) ——————————————————————

C) ——————————————————————————————

D) —————————

7.4) If each square is 1 feet square what is the area following figure occupies?

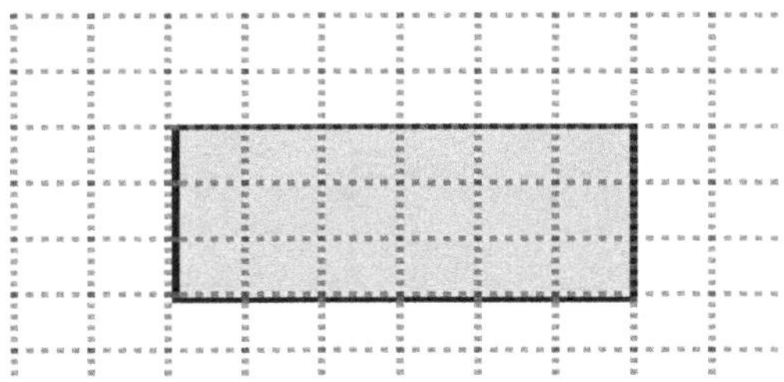

7.5) What is the difference in inches between the length of these two figures. Your answer should be to the ½ inch.

7.6) My mom placed a turkey in the oven at 1:45. 30 minutes later she put a pie in the same oven. She cooked both at the same time for 45 minutes. What time did she take both the turkey and pie from the oven?

7.7) On a fishing trip your family catches 50 fish then throws 15 back. Which number lone would be best in determining the number of fish your family kept.

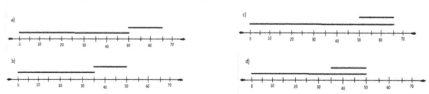

7.8) Michelle studies math from 3:15 p.m. to 6:45 p.m. Which clock shows a time that she would be studying.

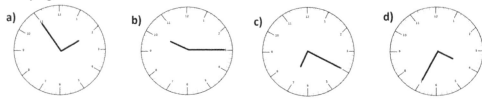

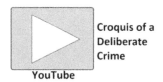

Croquis of a
Deliberate
Crime

YouTube

For one on one tutoring via skype at $35.00/Hr.; contact me at marksmathtutoring@yahoo.com

7.9) The two clocks below show what time I started jogging and them stopped

STARTED   FINISHED

Which digital clock below shows a time of day I would have been jogging

a)   b)   c)   d)

 4:35   6:45   3:35   11:45

7.10) Mom put a turkey and a pie in the oven. They both went in at 4:15. The pie finished at 5:30. The turkey went an additional 45 minutes. Which clock below show the time the turkey was finished?

a)    b)   c)   d)

7.11) which letter best represents a point at 115?

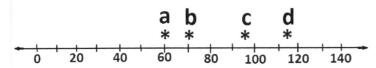

7.12) Which number best represents the dot in the plot below

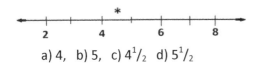

a) 4,   b) 5,   c) $4^1/_2$ d) $5^1/_2$

7.13) Which thermometer below show the temperature of 69^0F

a)   b)   c)   d)

7.14) What Is the temperature shown below   7.15) What is the temperature shown below

7.16) What is the temperature shown below

7.17) What is the temperature shown below

7.18) what is the value of the point in the diagram below

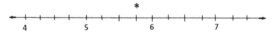

a) $6^1/_4$, b) $6^3/_4$, c) $5^3/_4$, d) $5^1/_4$

7.19) Given the number line below,

Which stament below is correct
a) The dot has a value is more than 300
b) The dot has a value of less than 200
c) The dot has a value closer to 300 than 200
d) The dot has a value closer to 200 than 300

7.20) Given the number line below

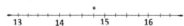

The is the correct value of the dot
a) $14^1/_4$, b) $15^3/_4$, c) $14^3/_4$, d) $15^1/_4$

7.21) Which number line best represents the value of ½ foot
a)   c)

7.22) What number best represents the dot on the following diagram

a) 275, b) 325, c) 225, d) 250

7.23) What are the vaues of the dots shown on the ruler below

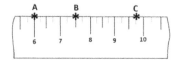

a) A=6, B=$7^1/_2$, C=$9^3/_4$
b) A=6, B=$7^1/_2$, C=$9^1/_4$
c) A=$6^1/_2$, B=$7^1/_2$, C=$9^3/_4$
d) A=6, B=$6^1/_2$, C=$9^1/_4$

7.24) The dot on the following number line represents a fraction

Which of the follwing number lines represents the same fraction

a)

c)

b)

d)

7.25) Which letter on the diagram below best represtents the number 243?

a) A
b) B
c) C
d) D

7.26) Which letter in the diagram below best represtnes the number 18 $^3/_4$

a) M
b) N
c) O
d) P

7.27) The R on the number line below is what value?

a) 13 ½
b) 12 ¾
c) 13 ¾
d) 12 ½

7.28) What is the best value for the letter R in the number line below?

a) 719
b) 715
c) 723
d) 727

7.29) The letter U in the diagram below best representes what number?

a) 15.1
b) 14.9
c) 14.7
d) 15.2

7.30) The letter T in the number line below beast represents what number

a) 32
b) 32.1
c) 31.9
d) 31.8

7.44) Use a ruler, what is the perimiter of this draqwing to ½ inch

7.45) Use a ruler to measure the perimiters of the two following shapes. What is the difference in their perimiters to ½ inch?

7.46) What is the temp shown below?

7.47) What is the temp shown below?

7.48) Use a ruler. What is the length on the line drawn below in centimeters to ½ centimeter?

7.49) Use a ruler. What is the length on the line drawn below in centimeters to ½ centimeter?

7.50) Use a ruler. What is the length on the line drawn below in centimeters to ½ centimeter?

Croquis of a
Deliberate
Crime
YouTube

If you don't get the correct answer, and want an explanation on how to work the problem, go to YouTube and type in "MMT" then the problem number. An example would be, MMT 3.9.w12,. The video will show you how to work problem 3.9.w12.

For one on one tutoring via skype at $35.00/Hr.; contact me at marksmathtutoring@yahoo.com

8.0 STATS

8.1) Roger has marbles in a bag, with the following colors and quantities.

COLOR	QUANTITY
Red	10
Blue	15
Green	10
White	5
Brown	20

If Roger picks a marble at random what are the odds of it being a Red one
a) 10 in 60, b) 10 in 50, c) 50 in 60, d) 15 in 60

8.2) Given the diagram below

☐ ☐ ☐ ☐ ○
☐ ☐ ☐ ☐ ○

If I pick a shape at random without looking what are the odds it will be a square
a) 8 out of 10, b) 2 out of 10, c) 3 out of 5, d) 2 out of 5

8.3) Given the table below describing the types of cookies in a box

COOKIE TYPE	QUANTITY
Sugar	17
Oatmeal	15
Chocolate	20
Mint	17
Cinnamon	13

If I pick a cookie at random without looking what two types of cookies will have the same odds of being picked?

8.4) Pam has 18 brown marbles, 12 Green marbles, and 21 white marbles in a bag. If she chooses one at random without looking which statement below is true?
a) She will pick a brown one for sure
b) She is less likely to pick a Green one than a Brown
c) She is more likely to pick a Brown than a White
d) It is impossible to pick a Green marble

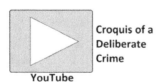

Croquis of a
Deliberate
Crime

YouTube

If you don't get the correct answer, and want an explanation on how to work the problem, go to YouTube and type in "MMT" then the problem number. An example would be, MMT 3.9.w12,. The video will show you how to work problem 3.9.w12.

For one on one tutoring via skype at $35.00/Hr.; contact me at marksmathtutoring@yahoo.com

100 SECTION ANSWER KEY

2.0 Logic

2.1) B	2.2) D	2.3) C	2.4) C	2.5) B	2.6) D	2.7) 1
2.8) 7	2.9) C	2.10) C	2.11) B	2.12) B	2.13) A	2.14) B
2.15) A	2.16) A	2.17) A	2.18) 16, 32, 94		2.19) C	2.20) A
2.21) D	2.29) D	2.30) D	2.35) B	2.36) A	2.37) D	

3.1 Addition Single Digit

3.1.1) 4	3.1.2) 2	3.1.3) 10	3.1.4) 13	3.1.5) 5	3.1.6) 10
3.1.7) 3	3.1.8) 16	3.1.9) 9	3.1.10) 10	3.1.11) 11	3.1.12) 8
3.1.13) 9	3.1.14) 14	3.1.15) 7	3.1.16) 15	3.1.17) 6	3.1.18) 11
3.1.19) 4	3.1.20) 12	3.1.21) 10	3.1.22) 14	3.1.23) 10	3.1.24) 13
3.1.25) 11	3.1.26) 15	3.1.27) 18	3.1.28) 9	3.1.29) 12	3.1.30) 9
3.1.31) 3	3.1.32) 15	3.1.33) 8	3.1.34) 7	3.1.35) 13	3.1.36) 6
3.1.37) 13	3.1.38) 16	3.1.39) 15	3.1.40) 7	3.1.41) 11	3.1.42) 11
3.1.43) 10	3.1.44) 13	3.1.45) 9	3.1.46) 14	3.1.47) 13	3.1.48) 12
3.1.49) 16	3.1.50) 9	3.1.51) 10	3.1.52) 14	3.1.53) 5	3.1.54) 11

3.2 Addition Two Digit

3.2.1) 34	3.2.2) 42	3.2.3) 50	3.2.4) 133	3.2.5) 105	3.2.6) 93
3.2.7) 56	3.2.8) 129	3.2.9) 70	3.2.10) 111	3.2.11) 59	3.2.12) 124
3.2.13) 107	3.2.14) 65	3.2.15) 136	3.2.16) 104	3.2.17) 72	3.2.18) 60
3.2.19) 74	3.2.20) 90	3.2.21) 151	3.2.22) 125	3.2.23) 88	3.2.24) 59
3.2.25) 108	3.2.26) 73	3.2.27) 85	3.2.28) 88	3.2.29) 87	3.2.30) 133
3.2.31) 83	3.2.32) 106	3.2.33) 105	3.2.34) 87	3.2.35) 111	3.2.36) 71
3.2.37) 55	3.2.38) 113	3.2.39) 121	3.2.40) 132	3.2.41) 164	3.2.42) 68
3.2.43) 121	3.2.44) 143	3.2.45) 120	3.2.46) 136	3.2.47) 55	3.2.48) 129

3.3 Addition Multiple Digit Addition

3.3.1) 2476	3.3.2) 2428	3.3.3) 503	3.3.4) 6990	3.3.5) 8323	3.3.6) 933
3.3.7) 1814	3.3.8) 1294	3.3.9) 6628	3.3.10) 1118	3.3.11) 600	3.3.12) 1253
3.3.13) 1081	3.3.14) 1065	3.3.15) 236	3.3.16) 1048	3.3.17) 732	3.3.18) 416
3.3.19) 974	3.3.20) 590	3.3.21) 651	3.3.22) 1025	3.3.23) 2288	3.3.24) 528
3.3.25) 531	3.3.26) 737	3.3.27) 861	3.3.28) 897	3.3.29) 878	3.3.30) 1333
3.3.31) 836	3.3.32) 1070	3.3.33) 1058	3.3.34) 5925	3.3.35) 11215	3.3.36) 589
3.3.37) 914	3.3.38) 3455	3.3.39) 1980	3.3.40) 1460	3.3.41) 3380	3.3.42) 276
3.3.43) 221	3.3.44) 643	3.3.45) 1120	3.3.46) 536		

3.3.w1) 1078 3.3.w2) 749 3.3.w3) 197 3.3.w4) 499 3.3.w5) 82 3.3.w6) 17
3.3.w7) 129 3.3.w8) 305 3.3.w9) 157 3.3.w10) 784 3.3.w11) 627 3.3.w12) 22, 26
3.3.w13) 44 3.3.w14) A 3.3.w15) $690 3.3.w16) $44.05 3.3.w17) 1195
3.3.w22) C 3.3.w23) B 3.3.w24) A

3.4 Subtraction Single Digits

3.4.1) 2 3.4.2) 2 3.4.3) 2 3.4.4) 1 3.4.5) 1 3.4.6) 4
3.4.7) 3 3.4.8) 3 3.4.9) 0 3.4.10) 1 3.4.11) 3 3.4.12) 1
3.4.13) 1 3.4.14) 1 3.4.15) 1 3.4.16) 3 3.4.17) 1 3.4.18) 1
3.4.19) 0 3.4.20) 3 3.4.21) 6 3.4.22) 4 3.4.23) 2 3.4.24) 3
3.4.25) 1 3.4.26) 1 3.4.27) 0 3.4.28) 9 3.4.29) 0 3.4.30) 2
3.4.31) 7 3.4.32) 1 3.4.33) 4 3.4.34) 4 3.4.35) 5 3.4.36) 3
3.4.37) 1 3.4.38) 0 3.4.39) 3 3.4.40) 3 3.4.41) 1 3.4.42) 7
3.4.43) 4 3.4.44) 5 3.4.45) 2 3.4.46) 0 3.4.47) 3 3.4.48) 2
3.4.49) 0 3.4.50) 5 3.4.51) 2 3.4.52) 0 3.4.53) 1 3.4.54) 2

3.5 Subtraction of Two Digits

3.5.1) 58 3.5.2) 2 3.5.3) 18 3.5.4) 37 3.5.5) 61 3.5.6) 13
3.5.7) 58 3.5.8) 33 3.5.9) 60 3.5.10) 13 3.5.11) 9 3.5.12) 46
3.5.13) 67 3.5.14) 7 3.5.15) 32 3.5.16) 90 3.5.17) 16 3.5.18) 56
3.5.19) 4 3.5.20) 32 3.5.21) 17 3.5.22) 71 3.5.23) 30 3.5.24) 39
3.5.25) 30 3.5.26) 51 3.5.27) 9 3.5.28) 74 3.5.29) 19 3.5.30) 25
3.5.31) 21 3.5.32) 9 3.5.33) 53 3.5.34) 25 3.5.35) 1 3.5.36) 9
3.5.37) 47 3.5.38) 51 3.5.39) 57 3.5.40) 18 3.5.41) 8 3.5.42) 44
3.5.43) 29 3.5.44) 61 3.5.45) 14 3.5.46) 62 3.5.47) 9 3.5.48) 29

3.6 Subtraction Multiple Digit

3.6.1) 746 3.6.2) 2026 3.6.3) 183 3.6.4) 140 3.6.5) 8279 3.6.6) 1029
3.6.7) 1736 3.6.8) 328 3.6.9) 6418 3.6.10) 234 3.6.11) 90 3.6.12) 755
3.6.13) 371 3.6.14) 67 3.6.15) 52 3.6.16) 792 3.6.17) 158 3.6.18) 272
3.6.19) 264 3.6.20) 82 3.6.21) 117 3.6.22) 71 3.6.23) 970 3.6.24) 110
3.6.25) 199 3.6.26) 483 3.6.27) 89 3.6.28) 639 3.6.29) 194 3.6.30) 247
3.6.31) 414 3.6.32) 594 3.6.33) 528 3.6.34) 4703 3.6.35) 1113 3.6.36) 53
3.6.37) 1038 3.6.38) 58 3.6.39) 138 3.6.40) 1034 3.6.41) 228 3.6.42) 2823
3.6.43) 1326 3.6.44) 102 3.6.45) 3132 3.6.46) 57 3.6.47) 214 3.6.48) 129
3.6.49) 191 3.6.50) 144 3.6.51) 2862 3.6.52) 38

3.6.w1) A 3.6.w2) 99 3.6.w3) 29 3.6.w4) 44 3.6.w5) 1568 3.6.w6) A
3.6.w7) B 3.6.w8) 154 3.6.w9) A 3.6.w10) 474 3.6.w11) C 3.6.w12) 15
3.6.w13) 9353 3.6.w14) A 3.6.w15) 18850 3.6.w16) $4.50
3.6.w17) $10.76 3.6.w180 $7.88 3.6.w19) 88 3.6.w24) 261

3.7 Multiplication of Single Digits

3.7.1) 3	3.7.2) 0	3.7.3) 24	3.7.4) 40	3.7.5) 6	3.7.6) 21
3.7.7) 0	3.7.8) 63	3.7.9) 8	3.7.10) 25	3.7.11) 28	3.7.12) 12
3.7.13) 20	3.7.14) 45	3.7.15) 10	3.7.16) 54	3.7.17) 8	3.7.18) 24
3.7.19) 4	3.7.20) 32	3.7.21) 16	3.7.22) 45	3.7.23) 24	3.7.24) 40
3.7.25) 28	3.7.26) 56	3.7.27) 81	3.7.28) 0	3.7.29) 36	3.7.30) 14
3.7.31) 2	3.7.32) 56	3.7.33) 12	3.7.34) 12	3.7.35) 36	3.7.36) 5
3.7.37) 42	3.7.38) 64	3.7.39) 54	3.7.40) 6	3.7.41) 30	3.7.42) 18
3.7.43) 21	3.7.44) 36	3.7.45) 18	3.7.46) 45	3.7.47) 40	3.7.48) 35
3.7.49) 64	3.7.50) 14	3.7.51) 24	3.7.52) 49	3.7.53) 6	3.7.54) 18

3.8 Multiplication of Two Digit

3.8.1) 253	3.8.2) 440	3.8.3) 544	3.8.4) 4420	3.8.5) 1826	3.8.6) 1980
3.8.7) 663	3.8.8) 3888	3.8.9) 325	3.8.10) 2738	3.8.11) 850	3.8.12) 3315
3.8.13) 2520	3.8.14) 784	3.8.15) 4048	3.8.16) 1104	3.8.17) 1232	3.8.18) 896
3.8.19) 1045	3.8.20) 1944	3.8.21) 5628	3.8.22) 2646	3.8.23) 1711	3.8.24) 760
3.8.25) 2376	3.8.26) 682	3.8.27) 1786	3.8.28) 912	3.8.29) 1472	3.8.30) 4266
3.8.31) 1702	3.8.32) 1584	3.8.33) 2054	3.8.34) 1736	3.8.35) 2210	3.8.36) 1344
3.8.37) 714	3.8.38) 3192	3.8.39) 2848	3.8.40) 4355	3.8.41) 6723	3.8.42) 1431
3.8.43) 1395	3.8.44) 3450	3.8.45) 5092	3.8.46) 2812	3.8.47) 3663	3.8.48) 4368

3.9 Multiplication Multi Digit

3.9.1) 262,515	3.9.2) 447,627	3.9.3) 54,880	3.9.4) 1,126,125
3.9.5) 182,622	3.9.6) 199,262	3.9.7) 69,225	3.9.8) 391,713
3.9.9) 684,915	3.9.10) 278,992	3.9.11) 87,975	3.9.12) 340,746
3.9.13) 257,730	3.9.14) 110,084	3.9.15) 8448	3.9.16) 117,760
3.9.17) 127,715	3.9.18) 37,488	3.9.19) 101,745	3.9.20) 85,344
3.9.21) 104,228	3.9.22) 216,646	3.9.23) 65,511	3.9.24) 48,671
3.9.25) 60,590	3.9.26) 68,970	3.9.27) 183,350	3.9.28) 99,072
3.9.29) 151,512	3.9.30) 428,970	3.9.31) 172,875	3.9.32) 161,616
3.9.34) 210,145	3.9.35) 1,761,854	3.9.36) 22,779,864	3.9.37) 11,928
3.9.38) 195,853	3.9.39) 1,635,174	3.9.40) 540,531	3.9.41) 530,299
3.9.42) 403,744	3.9.43) 7595	3.9.44) 8050	3.9.45) 100,392
3.9.46) 130,416	3.9.47) 67,063		

3.9.w1) 24	3.9.w2) 42	3.9.w3) 6	3.9.w4) 24	3.9.w5) 42	3.9.w6) C
3.9.w7) 72	3.9.w8) 7	3.9.w9) 63	3.9.w10) 4	3.9.w11) B	3.9.w12) C
3.9.w13) D	3.9.w14)584	3.9.w15) 36	3.9.w16) 768	3.9.w17)315	3.9.w18) B
3.9.w19) B	3.9.w20) B	3.9.w21) 72	3.9.w22) 18	3.9.w23) 35	3.9.w24) 48
3.9.w25) B	3.9.w26) B	3.9.w27) A	3.9.w28) C	3.9.w29) C	3.9.w31) C
3.9.w32) 384	3.9.w33) 592	3.9.w34) 6900	3.9.w35) 4032	3.9.w36) B	3.9.w37) 900
3.9.w38) 4800	3.9.w39) D	3.9.w41) B	3.9.w42) 1904		3.9.W43) $12,500
3.9.w44) 1176	3.9.w45) 48	3.9.w46) C	3.9.w48) B		

3.10 Division-no remanders

3.10.1) 2	3.10.2) 1	3.10.3) 3	3.10.4) 1	3.10.5) 4	3.10.6) 2
3.10.7) 1	3.10.8) 5	3.10.9) 1	3.10.10) 6	3.10.11) 3	3.10.12) 2
3.10.13) 1	3.10.14) 7	3.10.15) 1	3.10.16) 8	3.10.17) 4	3.10.18) 2
3.10.19) 1	3.10.20) 9	3.10.21) 3	3.10.22) 1	3.10.23) 10	3.10.24) 5
3.10.25) 2	3.10.26) 1	3.10.27) 12	3.10.28) 6	3.10.29) 4	3.10.30) 3
3.10.31) 2	3.10.32) 1	3.10.33) 14	3.10.34) 7	3.10.35) 2	3.10.36) 1
3.10.37) 15	3.10.38) 5	3.10.39) 3	3.10.40) 1	3.10.41) 6	3.10.42)3
3.10.43) 10	3.10.44) 3	3.10.45) 3	3.10.46) 3	3.10.47) 2	3.10.48) 5
3.10.49) 1	3.10.50) 4	3.10.51) 2	3.10.52)1	3.10.53) 4	3.10.54) 1

3.10.w1) 4	3.10.w2)4	3.10.w3) 0	3.10.w4) 3	3.10.w5) 7	3.10.w6) 5
3.10.w7) A	3.10.w8) 7	3.10.w9) A	3.10.w10) B	3.10.w11) A	3.10.w12) B
3.10.w13) C	3.10.w14) B	3.10.w15) A			

3.11 Inequalities

3.11.1) F	3.11.2) F	3.11.3) T	3.11.4) F	3.11.5) T	3.11.6) F
3.11.7) F	3.11.8) T	3.11.9) T	3.11.10) F	3.11.11) T	3.11.12) F
3.11.13) T	3.11.14) T	3.11.15) F	3.11.16) F	3.11.17) F	3.11.18) T
3.11.19) T	3.11.20) F	3.11.21) T	3.11.22) F	3.11.23) F	3.11.24) F

3.11.w1) A	3.11.w2) D	3.11.w3) D	3.11.w4) D	3.11.w5) C	3.11.w6) B
3.11.w7) C	3.11.w8) C	3.11.w9) C			

4.1 Geometry

4.1) D	4.2) C	4.3) A, B, E, F, G		4.4) C	4.5) B
4.6) A	4.7) D	4.8) 9	4.9) 15	4.10) 18	4.11) 21
4.12) B	4.13) A	4.14) 6	4.15) 120	4.16) 76	4.17) No
4.18) C	4.19) A	4.20) YES	4.21) C	4.22) D	4.23) 4
4.24) 17	4.25) 22	4.26) 4	4.27) B	4.28) 28	4.29) 36M
4.30) B	4.31) 153	4.32) 69	4.33) B	4.34) A	4.35) B
4.36) A	4.37) D	4.38) D	4.39) C	4.40)B	4.41) 8
4.42) 10	4.55) 52	4.56) 156	4.61) D	4.62) D	4.63) A
4.64) B	4.65) D	4.66) C	4.67) C	4.68) A	4.69) A
4.70) D					

Croquis of a Deliberate Crime
YouTube

For one on one tutoring via skype at $35.00/Hr.; contact me at marksmathtutoring@yahoo.com

5.0 Fractions

5.1   5.2)   5.3)   5.4)

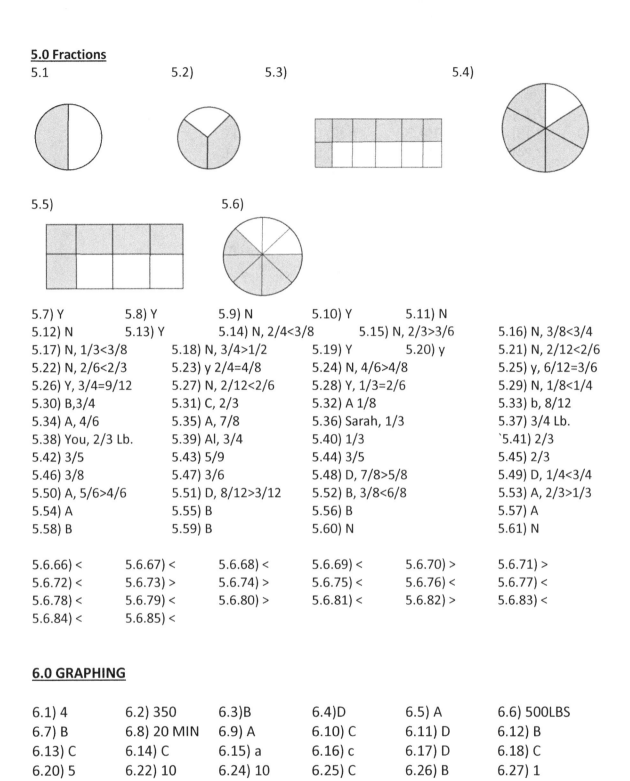

5.5)   5.6)

5.7) Y   5.8) Y   5.9) N   5.10) Y   5.11) N
5.12) N   5.13) Y   5.14) N, 2/4<3/8   5.15) N, 2/3>3/6   5.16) N, 3/8<3/4
5.17) N, 1/3<3/8   5.18) N, 3/4>1/2   5.19) Y   5.20) y   5.21) N, 2/12<2/6
5.22) N, 2/6<2/3   5.23) y 2/4=4/8   5.24) N, 4/6>4/8   5.25) y, 6/12=3/6
5.26) Y, 3/4=9/12   5.27) N, 2/12<2/6   5.28) Y, 1/3=2/6   5.29) N, 1/8<1/4
5.30) B,3/4   5.31) C, 2/3   5.32) A 1/8   5.33) b, 8/12
5.34) A, 4/6   5.35) A, 7/8   5.36) Sarah, 1/3   5.37) 3/4 Lb.
5.38) You, 2/3 Lb.   5.39) Al, 3/4   5.40) 1/3   `5.41) 2/3
5.42) 3/5   5.43) 5/9   5.44) 3/5   5.45) 2/3
5.46) 3/8   5.47) 3/6   5.48) D, 7/8>5/8   5.49) D, 1/4<3/4
5.50) A, 5/6>4/6   5.51) D, 8/12>3/12   5.52) B, 3/8<6/8   5.53) A, 2/3>1/3
5.54) A   5.55) B   5.56) B   5.57) A
5.58) B   5.59) B   5.60) N   5.61) N

5.6.66) <   5.6.67) <   5.6.68) <   5.6.69) <   5.6.70) >   5.6.71) >
5.6.72) <   5.6.73) >   5.6.74) >   5.6.75) <   5.6.76) <   5.6.77) <
5.6.78) <   5.6.79) <   5.6.80) >   5.6.81) <   5.6.82) >   5.6.83) <
5.6.84) <   5.6.85) <

6.0 GRAPHING

6.1) 4   6.2) 350   6.3)B   6.4)D   6.5) A   6.6) 500LBS
6.7) B   6.8) 20 MIN   6.9) A   6.10) C   6.11) D   6.12) B
6.13) C   6.14) C   6.15) a   6.16) c   6.17) D   6.18) C
6.20) 5   6.22) 10   6.24) 10   6.25) C   6.26) B   6.27) 1
6.30) D

If you don't get the correct answer, and want an explanation on how to work the problem, go to youtube and type in "MMT" then the problem number. An example would be "MMT 3.9.w12" The video will show you how to work problem 3.9.w12.

7.0 MEASURING

7.1) 3 CM	7.2) 6IN	7.3) A=1IN, B=2IN, C=$2^1/_2$IN, D=$^1/_2$ IN			7.4) 18
7.5) ½ IN	7.6) 3:00	7.7) D	7.8) D	7.9) B	7.10) 30
7.11) D	7.12) C	7.13) B	7.14) 96	7.15) 175	7.16) 17
7.17) 340	7.18) C	7.19) C	7.20) C	7.21) C	7.22) D
7.23) A	7.24) B	7.25) C	7.26) D	7.27) C	7.28) A
7.29) A	7.30) C	7.44)	7.45)	7.46) 92.5	7.47) 77.5
7.48) 1	7.49) 1 ½	7.50) 3 ½			

8.0 STATISTICS

8.1)A	8.2) A	8.3) Sugar and Mint	8.4) B

Croquis of a
Deliberate
Crime

YouTube

If you don't get the correct answer, and want an explanation on how to work the problem, go to YouTube and type in "MMT" then the problem number. An example would be, MMT 3.9.w12,. The video will show you how to work problem 3.9.w12.

For one on one tutoring via skype at $35.00/Hr.; contact me at marksmathtutoring@yahoo.com

Made in the USA
Monee, IL
05 September 2019